SLUGG

*A Boy's Life in the Age
of Mass Incarceration*

TONY LEWIS JR

WITH K.L. REEVES

Hanover Place Press
Washington, D.C.

Published by Hanover Place Press, Washington, D.C.

To Menina

Author's Note

Slugg was written between 2012 and 2013. It captures moments from my life up until the birth of my daughter. Significant events that align with this book's mission, from the nascent steps toward prison reform to the Black Lives Matter movement, have happened since the completion of the work. I have remained on the frontline of the fight and have had many experiences worth relating since I finished *Slugg*. I was tempted to go back and include some of those new encounters here, but I thought better of it. The spirit remains the same, and for all things there's a season. I hope you enjoy the seasons of my life represented in these pages.

Tony Lewis Jr.

Table of Contents

The Run

By the age of nineteen, my father had made more than a million dollars selling drugs. We were living in Largo, Maryland, in 1982, and I was two years old. In those days, my dad, Tony, Sr., had been buying other houses and apartments in the D.C. area, one being his apartment in Crystal City, Virginia. He didn't have as much need to stay at that apartment early on, but that would change as I got older and my mother and father's fights became more intense.

My parents grew up on the same block, Hanover Place, in northwest Washington, D.C. My mother lived on one side of Hanover, where poor black families owned row homes, and my father lived on the other side of the street where poorer black families were packed in cramped rat- and roach-infested two-bedroom apartments. In my father's family's apartment, one large rat would nightly crawl up and down the drainage pipe in their kitchen, and the sound of its claws against the metal made it difficult for my father to fall asleep. When he wasn't listening to the rats scurrying about in the apartment, he'd lie in bed imagining what it felt like to go to sleep with a full stomach or what it felt like not having holes in your shoes or how it felt to wear fine clothes.

I felt none of my parents' struggles in my earliest years. I was a pampered child. Still, I was bred tough and, naturally, was raised by my dad to love the sport of boxing. Not long after I started walking, he bought me a pair of red Sugar Ray Leonard boxing gloves. Sugar Ray's signature was scrawled atop the white bands on the wrists. He was from D.C., so he was our man. I loved those gloves. I remember running around our house with them coming up to my elbows. I can still feel my hands, hot and sweating, inside them.

By the age of four, I had long been taking my boxing gloves with me to Hanover. My extended family still lived there, but the conditions hadn't changed much since my parents were children, and the kids on the block were rough. I'd fight with them all, especially my first cousins Rico and Antonio. Rico and Antonio were five and six years older than me and helped me to get sharp early, hitting me with strong, playful blows and showing me how to bob and weave just like they had been taught by a local professional boxer.

As I got older and more skilled, my father and uncles started matching me up against children around my age and, every time they did, I'd win. So my dad started calling me Slugger. Eventually, he just shortened it to Slugg, and soon all the males around Hanover, young and old, started calling to me by that name. They'd say, "What's up, Slugg? Slugg, what's happening?" To this day, none of them call me Tony.

As a small child, I knew that everyone that mattered to me in the world would be around Hanover. Hanover's a short, narrow, one-way street tucked away in between 1st Street to the west, O Street to the north, and North Capitol Street to the east. To get to it, you have to come through a series of alleys, which protected us from outsiders, enemies, and the police. I'd be there nearly every day. Even when we lived in Maryland, Hanover always felt like home.

When my mother would drive us through that familiar alley pathway, I'd start bouncing in my seat. We were about to see family; that's where my dad would be and his side of the family: his mother, whom we called Lou, Aunt Maxine, Aunt Brenda, Uncle Bobby, Uncle Tyrone, Aunt Barbara, and all of my cousins. That's where my mother's mother, Grandma, lived, and where her big sister Aunt Bonnie would be, and her brothers, Uncle Alvin and Uncle Boo. My mother's other brother, Uncle Greg, was in prison back then.

When we'd arrive on Hanover, my dad was the first person I'd look for. But for a small child, finding him on the street was no easy task. Hanover was always crowded and loud. Imagine long lines of people like those at a grocery store just before the first flakes of a record snowstorm or lines like those at an amusement park at the newest or most-popular attraction. But instead of anticipating buying food or waiting for a thrilling ride, the people lined up on Hanover were there to buy cocaine. Most were users, but some were dealers. Of course, I didn't know the specifics then, but as I made my way through the maze, with my mother yelling "Tony!" to my father to let him know that I was on my way, I knew Cornell Jones was the man

11

and my father was the man next to the man.

On the way to him, I'd look up and see the rooftops patrolled by men like Black Wilson, Dan-Dan, or Lo. They'd be up
there watching for the police and stick-up boys. Older kids like
Earnest, Moe-Man, Mark, and Ju-Ju would go to the store for
the men on their post, finding their way up to the rooftop and
staying, anticipating who among them would be the first to yell
"Olleray!" when the police turned into the block off North
Capitol Street. Rico and Antonio would also be on the roof
sometimes. They'd see the police coming and they'd yell "Olleray!" Us children playing on the street would hear them and
excitedly echo the call, "Olleray! Olleray!"

"Olleray" is pig Latin for "roller," which was one of the many
names the police were given. Another popular one on Hanover
was "jump out" or "jump outs," which was a direct reference to
the way the police entered the block and hopped out of their
cars.

The children on Hanover helped to be lookouts out of a
sense of pride, not pointed duty. My father never told his
nephews and the other children on the block to climb the roof
and look out for the police. This was adaptive behavior. It's the
same sort of thing that led my father to hang around Uncle
Boo's crap games and run errands for all the men playing. You
created a role for yourself on the block, a way to work with
hopes that you'd be rewarded. To a boy with no male role
model at home, any form of acknowledgment from the strong
men on the block—a pat on the head, a "good job youngin'"—is

12

reward enough.

I shouted "olleray" for similar but also very different reasons. I was very young, yet I clearly remember shouting that word of caution and feeling proud. I was helping. I was assisting my father and his friends. While I didn't appreciate the full dynamics of all that was happening around me, fundamentally I knew I was helping. I was helping the man who acknowledged me, affirmed me, and loved me daily, and by echoing the other children's screams of caution, I was returning that love.

Along with the drug lines, the maze of people I had to make my way through as a child consisted primarily of people buying things, selling things, and just hanging out. Hanover wasn't simply one of the largest open-air drug markets in the country; it was also a market for stolen or hijacked goods. I remember playing outside on the block and never being able to see to the end of the street because of the crowds of people. The atmosphere made our short street feel like Chicago's Magnificent Mile or Fifth Avenue in Midtown Manhattan during the Christmas rush. It was like that every day: long lines that lengthened on the weekends and around the first of the month, combined with a whole other mass of people and peddlers. The boosters and hijackers would come to Hanover every day and set up shop. They'd bring diamond rings, big screen TVs, fur coats, furniture sets, refrigerators, and washers and dryers. There'd be stereo systems, VCRs, and VHS tapes, cassette tapes, rugs, china sets, tires, bikes, toys, and anything else you can think of.

On warm days, everyone would be outside, kids playing in

the street, people relaxing on their porches or in their back-yards, holding card games until all hours of the night. There'd be dice games going with piles of money on the pavement, and the older women from the block would prepare their signature dishes like crab cakes and fried crab to sell.

My father was like the president and general manager of Cornell's drug operation. In an environment that could have easily been chaotic there was the highest order. Everyone knew his or her place, and very rarely did anyone step out of line. My father's men patrolled the lines with baseball bats, and I only remember seeing one person get beat up badly. After it hap-pened, I asked my dad why his men had beaten the man that way. He said to me, "Because he took something that didn't belong to him." As a child, I saw and heard all these things and interpreted them as a child accustomed to that life would, but I also made sense of them based on how my parents were raising me. I remember thinking, "Don't take what doesn't belong to you. Bad things will happen to you if you do."

We were safe on Hanover. The children played together among all that was going on. I boxed and learned to ride my bike and played freaky Friday, hot bread-n-butter, and countless other games on Hanover. But while many of my friends, even those that were the same age as me at the time, were free to run around, I had to remain always within eyesight of my mother and sometimes my father. Obviously, he was often busy. To the other children, particularly my cousins Rico and Antonio, my parents seemed strict, but aside from my father's

14

career as a drug dealer, they cared for me in the typical way any loving and responsible parent would. I should not have been so young and free to roam our neighborhood. Yet, unfortunately, many of the children in the neighborhood and many of my friends had this freedom.

A lot of people get their first jobs from a friend or a neighbor, working somewhere in close proximity to their home. My father did the same, except his block happened to specialize in crime. On Hanover, you got money illegally to take care of the necessities. And what begins out of a sense of desperation continues as a way of life.

For such a short period of prominence, cocaine had a profound effect on our lives. We lived with very little consciousness about the larger forces that contributed to the conditions of our environment. The whys are irrelevant when you're in it; you just get it, get what you can, get through the day, and hardly think about the next day. But now that my life is stable, I often reflect and look for answers about the conditions I had no answers for growing up.

I was born into the recession of the early 1980s, and my father saw continuing to hustle as the better choice to provide for me out of a few different criminal opportunities. The criminal life is never the only way; a way can be made out of no way through right living, patience, and prudence. But these character attributes are learned and take time to develop. No one starts out with them. They have to be taught. Unfortunately, the kind of value system from which they slowly emerge is rarely taught or practiced in the hood. So without the right support, young men from broken, fatherless homes, like my father, look to themselves. They look to their block and what's happening on their block to put money in their pocket. Often, what's happening is crime. When you're hungry, it doesn't feel like a decision, like a choice. It is survival: the instinct of self-preservation takes over. You go to the nearest opportunity. And as a teenager, my father saw opportunity with the older guys standing on the block selling weed.

Cornell Jones grew up on Hanover and used to hang with Uncle Boo and Uncle Greg. Cornell was Uncle Boo's age, and his older brother, Junie, was Uncle Greg's age. They were all into robbing banks when they were younger, but after doing some jail time, they all stopped—except Uncle Greg. Uncle Boo started gambling heavily, and Cornell started selling drugs.

At the time, selling drugs was a far less risky criminal affair, so Cornell got a group of guys from Hanover to sell sticks of weed for him. My father was nearly ten years younger than Cornell, so they weren't peers growing up, but they knew each other—everyone on Hanover did. Uncle Boo had gotten my father "off the porch," as the expression around our way goes. But Boo was a gambler, and your money has to be long to be a successful gambler. At the time, my father couldn't take the losses, so he looked to Cornell's operation as another way to support himself.

My father was much younger than everyone who was really

hustling and getting money, and he understood the order of things. So he didn't just approach Cornell and ask him for work. Also, by then, Cornell had moved off the block and only came around to check on his product and his workers, so he wasn't nearly as accessible. But his workers were, and my father knew that they didn't always like to be out there selling. If it was winter, or if there was a party or a concert they wanted to go to, they would often leave their posts. So my father approached them and asked them to leave the weed with him when they didn't want to be out there, and he'd sell it for them. They agreed to that arrangement, and he started hustling for them. There wasn't much money in it for my dad, but it was enough to feed himself and his siblings and enough to get by on.

On one particularly cold night, Cornell came around to check on things. He pulled up, called my father over to the car, and asked him where his workers were. My dad had recruited a friend of his named Abby who was in the same situation as him, and it was just the two of them out there. My dad told Cornell the older guys were gone, but he and Abby were selling for them. Cornell was surprised but pleased. He knew my father, and the product was still moving.

The arrangement continued as the older guys working for Cornell started to get more comfortable. They were making good money and could afford to pay my father a small portion of it for doing most of the work. So when Cornell came around to check on things, he saw my father and his friend out there more and more. Finally, one day someone within Cornell's crew stole a large portion of weed from one of the stash houses on the block. This enraged Cornell. Not caring who did it, he fired everyone who was working for him and put my father in charge in their place.

This was the true beginning of my father's drug-dealing career. In his new position of authority, he started making what he felt was an incredible amount of money, but it was nothing compared to the money he would make with the white stuff.

My father started dealing cocaine when Cornell Jones returned to prison for the second time in 1978. By that point, my dad had developed a reputation for himself as a capable street dude and drug dealer. So a much older hustler named Sonny Reds recruited him to sell cocaine for him on Hanover. This all happened with Uncle Boo's approval. Sonny Reds was an outsider, and Uncle Boo had to get a piece of the action from any outsider's operation happening on Hanover. At the start, my father was partnered with another man, but they fell out. Again, my dad was younger than everyone else, so the man kept trying to take advantage of him when it was time to settle on the money. Finally, my dad severed the partnership and started buying the drugs directly from Sonny Reds himself, despite being charged higher prices.

Cornell stayed in prison for about a year, and by the time he got out, my father had built up a substantial clientele. Having made some connections in prison, Cornell hit the street and quickly started up his operation again. But my father had his own thing working for Sonny Reds, so he and Cornell competed for a short while.

My dad had more customers when Cornell first got out, but over time, he noticed that he was losing some of them. Cornell had the superior product and a larger plan he was ready to put in place.

One day Cornell came around Hanover to check on things, and in the process went to find my father. When he found him, the two started talking, and at some point during the conversation, Cornell extended an offer to be his partner. He shared his vision for how things would be: they'd combine forces, Cornell would supply the product and my father would run the operation. It would be big, nothing compared to what they had going before. To my father it all sounded too good to be true, but he respected Cornell and decided to join him.

I attended private school throughout my elementary and secondary years of education. My father would drop me off at my school with me looking as neat, clean, and well put together as a little boy could look in his uniform. When he came to pick me up, however, I'd run to the car looking like a completely different boy with my clothes all out of place and disheveled. We had many of those moments, and though I don't remember them as well as he does, I know he was there with me. I hold that feeling. I was fortunate to have a relationship with my father. Most of my peers didn't know who their fathers were, or they had ghost dads, spectral figures who appeared infrequently and disappeared quickly; their presence haunted their children.

As a child, I couldn't perceive all the subtleties of the adult world, but the things that represented distinction I remember well. Perhaps this is because various people who I'd be around would make a big deal about the way my family was living. They would point it out to me, and it made me start paying attention. When I was young, I remember people around Hanover saying to me, "Your father's a hustler, shorty. He getting money!" They'd treat me differently because of who he was. I knew I was different, that we were different, and because of that, and the fact that I spent a lot of my time around adults, I matured with a heightened sense of awareness.

My parents, however, never made distinctions. They told me that I was special, but that I was not better than anyone else. They didn't make a show of the things that we did or the things we had, they just did it and had it and would often share it with our family. My father would talk to me about our good fortune and the importance of understanding that not everyone had it the way we did. At that time, he never talked about how hard he had it as a child, but I know now that this is partly where those conversations came from. I watched my father, Uncle Boo, and Cornell give so much of what they had to others that giving became a part of who I became. At the time, I didn't see, couldn't see, how the drugs my father and Cornell dealt impacted the community. Truthfully, while they were in it, neither could they, not in the larger way some learned person on the outside would see it. What I did see, daily, was how much these men gave. I saw them giving all the time—to family, to friends, to virtual strangers, and especially to children. Once a year, they got chartered buses and sent all the children on Hanover to places like Myrtle Beach and Disney World. They supported the neighborhood children in their athletics and extracurricular activities and encouraged them, genuinely, to do well in school, paying them for A's and B's.

As a boy, I watched and participated in the giving, and with that ingrained in me, I would freely give my things away too. I did it indiscriminately to the point where it would confuse my parents. They knew they'd raised me to be that way, but they also wanted me to have some things for myself. They, of course, kept things for themselves, many things.

I remember being asked in school what my father did for a living and having to make up a profession like firefighter or something. I'd respond in a matter-of-fact way like the other kids. I was from a crime family, and that was all I knew. Yet, as long as I can remember, I had sense enough to know that my father's work wasn't something that was to be shared with my classmates or my teacher. Still, given the way we lived, it was hard to hide.

I didn't get picked up from school the way the other children at my school got picked up. My elementary school was a good school, but it wasn't one that was known for its exclusivity, as my high school would be. I had few, if any, rich classmates, so imagine my father rolling in to pick me up at different times throughout the years in a Porsche 928 or a Porsche 944, the Mercedes Benz 560 coupe and the Mercedes 560 SL, the 735 BMW or his Range Rover. There were a few other cars, but those are the ones that stand out in my mind. Can you imagine what my teachers and my schoolmates' parents must have thought? Here's a young black man in his early to mid-twenties in the 1980s driving these types of automobiles, and on any given day, if he stepped out of one of these cars, he'd be dressed in high-end designer clothing, certainly with designer shoes on his feet, and sometimes designer shades on his face. We must have made quite the scene. They knew my father wasn't from a wealthy black family. They knew he wasn't a ballplayer. Hip-hop was still in its infancy, and few, if any, rappers possessed a fleet of luxury cars like that—and, anyway, he wasn't in entertainment. So they probably assumed he was doing something illegal, which he was. These are the kinds of things I think about now—how I saw the world and how the world saw me, us, back then. I was a child, and that was my life, my father pulling up to school in one of these cars or even sometimes a limousine, and me hopping in asking excitedly, "Dad, where are we going today?"

He and I were always going somewhere together, somewhere fun. If we were around town, we'd go shopping in Georgetown or at the Mazza Gallerie or White Flint Mall. We'd go get ice cream from Swensen's Ice Cream Parlor, and for dinner we'd eat regularly at places like Market Inn, Crisfield's, and Houston's. We had a dedicated parking spot for the Washington Bullets (now known as the Wizards) games, and though I was too young to attend the Washington Redskins Super Bowl victory in 1983, I did go with him when the 'Skins returned to the big game the following year in Tampa, Florida. We went to Vegas all the time together, a few times just him and me. My dad had a leather pouch where he held all his gambling money, and I'd be in charge of carrying it.

My father enjoyed gambling, and when he did gamble he'd bet big. With Atlantic City being only a few hours from D.C., we traveled there together regularly. Atlantic City was a place that I often went to with both of my parents. The three of us didn't take many trips together as a family, but Atlantic City was one of the places that brought us all together. Quite a few members of my extended family would travel with us too.

In June of 1988, a large group of my relatives drove to Atlantic City to see the Mike Tyson/Michael Spinks fight. It was a star-studded event built up to be a heavyweight contest for the ages. It became the highest-grossing fight of all time up until that point, yet it lasted not much longer than a minute. Tyson knocked Spinks out in ninety-one seconds.

I remember my father being visibly frustrated after the fight. Just he and I sat ringside for that one, but some of the other men in my family, including my cousins Kevin, Rico, and Antonio, in addition to some of my father's friends, were not too far away from us. My mother, Lou, and Aunt Barbara were in Atlantic City with us, but they watched the fight on television from the hotel. It was one of those trips where my dad treated the family for the entire weekend. Everyone's food, entertainment, and shopping was on him.

Spinks had never lost a professional bout and Tyson came into the night undefeated as well. The fight was billed as "once and for all," the crowning of the undisputed heavyweight champion because each fighter already had a heavyweight belt. I'll never forget my father's expression as he watched Spinks lying face up on the canvas and then struggling to get up on one knee only to fall back down through the ropes. With Spinks down and counted out, my father's look went from disbelief to anger. Outside of dealing with my mother, he rarely broke his cool, but by that ring in Atlantic City was one of those times. He had spent a lot of money on the tickets and the weekend in general, but I don't think it was the money that bothered him. More than others, my father lived in the ring with those fighters. His entire life had been a fight, and I think something inside of him wanted the fighters to battle, giving everything they had for the entire bout. There had to be a winner, and of the two Tyson was his man. Still, something inside of him wanted both fighters to take the blows, glancing and straight, and keep coming. Getting knocked down was all right, but you had to get back up on strong legs and fight, pushing through the dizzying uncertainty and the pain and using your toughness and wits to regain your senses and fight! Keep fighting and standing until the final bell rings and then, with the whole world watching, you've gained the respect of your opponent.

New York City was another place my parents and I frequented together. On those trips, my dad would usually take a limousine, and the three of us would ride up for all-day shopping sprees. I can't say I remember my parents ever being peaceful on those trips. They'd argue on the way up and they'd argue on the way down. Having purchased thousands of dollars' worth of merchandise didn't change anything. I remember us going to FAO Schwartz there. We had a smaller version of the toy store in D.C., but it was nothing compared to the flagship. I recall most vividly the toy soldier greeters at the entrance dressed in their bright red jackets and tall black hats, and the life-sized stuffed animals. For a little guy like me, it was toy heaven.

My father would often take the limousine around the city, too, but when he wanted to get away, sometimes he'd have his chauffeur, who also happened to be named Tony, drive him to New York. On one of those Tony-chauffeured trips to New York, my dad ordered a replica 560 SL Mercedes from FAO Schwartz for me. It was nearly the real thing, running on gas and equipped with a manual transmission. It must have cost a few thousand dollars. I sat in it but couldn't drive it. Actually, I never drove it. The car just remained in our basement, untouched for the most part except for once when Rico and Antonio and I were wrestling and I fell back into it, landing on the windshield and cracking it with my behind. The windshield wasn't real glass, but that was about the only part of the car that wasn't.

I had more things than any child could wish for. I remember

my mother giving away a refrigerator-sized box full of my clothes and shoes. It was all stuff I could still wear, designer stuff, but it didn't even put a dent in my wardrobe. I still had an embarrassing amount of clothes. We'd go shopping every day, but I learned early that having a lot of things meant nothing if you didn't have someone you loved and someone who loved you to share it with. I was often lonely as a child, and though my parents were great company, I relished the times that I could spend with children my age. I started to ask my dad if we could bring along one or more of my play pals in our travels. It was fun for me, but it also felt like a necessity to keep me from wither-ing away in boredom. Imagine being a child and going into a boutique alone with your dad and having to sit there for hours and watch him get tailored for dozens of Versace slacks and pants and shirts, and doing the same with other designers like Claude Montana and Gucci. Then the two of you going in and out of designer shoe stores, and him trying on and purchasing sixty some-odd pairs of shoes from designers like Susan Bennis and Warren Edwards. This happened regularly, and I wised up quick. So I'd ask my dad in advance if we could go pick up Rico and Antonio or my friend Scoop and sometimes my cousins, Kim and Alan, who were Uncle Boo's children. He never said no, and so from that point I learned to speak up. Shopping days or going to get a haircut or some of the other outings I considered boring were much more fun with my friends.

I used the same strategy with my mother at our house in Maryland. Given the way my parents had grown up, moving to the suburbs was a huge deal. My mother loved that house dearly. It was hers.

It was a three-bedroom split-level single-family home with a sizeable front yard and big backyard. When I wasn't playing outside with my friends, we'd usually be in the basement where there was plenty of room for us to run around. There was a laundry room down there, a full bar, a pool table, and a fireplace. We had one of those huge projector screen TVs with an audio system that included a turntable, dual cassette players, and a very early CD player, which I had no idea how to work and apparently neither did my mother because she never played CDs.

Upstairs in one of the guest rooms, we also had a computer, which no one ever touched. I learned later that my father had signed up for a computer course at one of the reputable computer learning schools of the time. He paid four thousand dollars for it but never attended. He also enrolled at the University of Maryland at College Park, signing up for a couple of business courses. His thought was that the schoolwork would help him transition from the drug business one day. But he could never stay awake for long in class, having been up all night in the streets. Once he had fallen asleep so deeply he didn't hear the lecture hall clearing when class was over. He awoke to the professor standing over him and telling him taking the course was a waste of his time if all he was going to do was sleep in it. He didn't return after that. It just wasn't a realistic endeavor given the life he was living. Both schools refunded portions of his tuition.

The importance of a formal education was never lost on either of my parents, though both had their own struggles with school. My father fought hard to finish high school. He was making a lot of money by the start of his senior year, and most of his friends had already dropped out, but something made him finish and receive his high school diploma. My mother, on the other hand, didn't finish high school. Still, she was the one that made all of the academic decisions for me, and she made them beautifully. She had a grand vision for my life, giving me two of the greatest gifts a person can receive: the gift of love—she loved me unconditionally—and the gift of literacy. It was she who introduced me to the wonders of the written word and taught me to read. I started reading early. I can't say exactly when, but I remember it being well before I began school. I walked into kindergarten well equipped because my mother read to me every night. She would even continue to spend time reading with me when I was able to read fluently myself.

Once I learned the magic of words, I went through a phase where I read aloud everything I saw. We'd be out and I'd read every sign, every marquee, every billboard, anything that had words strung together. I can still hear myself, just going, and feeling the great satisfaction of knowing. When I'd get stuck on words or phrases and couldn't work through them, my mother or father would help me through it. Sometimes they'd be driving and wouldn't see the sign or whatever it was I saw, but through the beginning of my words would help me complete what was missing. They never tired of me in this phase. I never heard from them to be quiet or equivalent words in much harsher terms. My mother cursed at me, but not in those moments, not when all I was doing was discovering. She cursed to reprimand me for doing something I shouldn't have done, or I'd hear her curse about other people. I see and hear parents in the hood cursing their children out for being children, for discovering, and it hurts my heart. I can only imagine what's starting to happen in their little heads. My mother let me discover, she led me and learned with me. She did the best she could with what she had, and that had nothing to do with money.

My mother's love had a powerful impact on my life. All those quiet times with just her and me in the house, they didn't seem like much at the time. And I can clearly remember episodes when I took our sessions for granted and when her insistent efforts toward forwarding my education frustrated me. For example, she had these flashcards that she'd drill me with. I'd get tired and want to do something else, but she wouldn't let me go. Most times, I got what I wanted and pretty much did what I wanted to do, but not those times. We'd have little arguments about it, and of course she'd win. And we wouldn't stop with those flashcards until she was satisfied.

I felt her love when she'd be in her room and I'd be in mine, and she'd come check on me to see if I was all right. Some of those times, those quiet times when she popped into my room, I'd beg her to take me over to Hanover. I also remember her checking in on me at night and getting me up to use the bathroom. These are little things, yet they are big things. My mother and I often discussed the value of honesty and morality, letting me know that I could talk to her about anything.

I remember us watching TV together, programs like *The Cosby Show, Knots Landing, Dynasty*, and *Dallas*. My mother was the best cook. Food was another one of those areas where my parents pampered me. Aside from our pantry bursting with junk food, my mother would cook anything I wanted or take me wherever I wanted to go to eat. The same went for my father, except for the cooking ability. The times that the three of us sat and ate dinner together happened with enough regularity to be one of our norms. I don't know the limits I'd go to have a moment today that even remotely resembles our once-ordinary dinners for three from yesterday.

I didn't make many friends in Maryland. And the only friend from around Hanover to come to our house was my best friend Scoop. When we were very young, Scoop lived in a housing project called Tyler House with his grandmother. Tyler House is very close to Hanover, just across New York Avenue. When I got to be old enough to leave my parents' eyesight, I remember crossing the busy New York Avenue to see Scoop. That journey itself always felt like an adventure.

But most of my play pals were my family members, especially in those early years. Uncle Alvin's sons Kevin and Don would come over to our house, and Aunt Barbara, who's not much older than me, would visit often. My cousin Kim, who is my age, and her brother Alan, who was three years younger than us, also came around a lot. And of course Rico and Antonio spent many nights. Out of the cousins I spent the most time around, Rico and Antonio had the least stable home. They lived with my father when they were boys, and my father then was just in his early teens. The three of them and the rest of the family, about ten people on average, all squeezed into the same cramped two-bedroom apartment that my father grew up in. The rats were still there, and, sleeping on the couch with his brother, Rico would be afraid to get up and go to the bathroom at night, so he'd lie there and wet himself instead.

Grandma Lou abandoned my father and his siblings early in their childhood, leaving them with a cruel, abusive stranger for a number of years. When she finally returned for her children, my father had become hardened toward her. Still, he loved his mother, and, a few years after he bought our place in Largo, he bought Lou a big house on the Gold Coast. I was there often because a lot of the family lived in that house, including Aunt Brenda, Aunt Barbara, and Rico and Antonio.

My father had a basketball court with two hoops built in the backyard of the house. One was a regulation hoop built in the half court, and the other was much shorter, built adjacent to it. The short one was my hoop. This was before adjustable rims, so my father had the contractors create a mini court off to the side for me.

When Rico and Antonio would come over to our house, my

mother treated them as if they were her own sons. She'd wash the clothes they had on and give them some of my clothes to wear. Rico and Antonio were among those with whom I shared so willingly. I was just so happy they were there! Sometimes my father would go pick them up and bring them over at night. I would wake up to them in my room and get up right away and we'd start playing. We did all the things children would do, and, of course, I had a lot of toys and playthings, video games and such, to play with. There was a time when my mother was reticent about me spending time with Rico and Antonio. My cousins were raised on Hanover with little guidance, like my father, so they were tough little boys. They were exposed to the same things that my parents had been exposed to, and my mother knew that. She wanted me to stay as innocent as possible for as long as possible, and she thought spending time close to them would take away some of my innocence. Playing outside in the street in front of Hanover was different. Sure, I picked up things there, but those times were filled with games, and the contact wasn't as intimate as being in a house. Plus, I was always in her sight, and she could quickly straighten out a situation if need be.

At the time, my mother didn't work, so my father took care of all the expenditures while my mother took care of her house. To this day, I don't think I've seen a house as impeccably kept up as our house in Maryland was. Our department store's worth of clothes were hung up, folded, and arranged as if they were on display. I can still see the top of my mother's closet lined neatly with a long row of designer purses by MCM, HCL, Gucci, and Fendi, and the other side stacked to the ceiling with shoeboxes by her favorite designers like Charles Jourdan and Joan & David.

Our carpet was always freshly vacuumed and scented, and all the tabletops, countertops, and anything that could collect dust or grime always shined. Our furniture was kept in pristine condition; if something started to show wear, she'd buy a new set.

Back then, I had a German Shepherd named Rambo. That dog frustrated my mother to no end, probably because my father bought him for me against my mother's wishes. The day he surprised me with it, I was staying over at Lou's. He brought Rambo in, and the puppy immediately started chasing me. I ran from it and hid under the kitchen table. My father laughed, saying, "You said you wanted a puppy, and now you scared of it." But it didn't take me long to get used to Rambo, and we played together the whole ride to our house in Maryland. I can still remember my mother cursing my father out when we walked in and she saw the puppy in my arms. But she could see that I had already taken to the pup and relented. Truly, I had everything I could have wanted.

One day my dad and I went shopping at Mazza Gallerie. It was a normal day, a relaxed day for the two of us. I was older, fast approaching my ninth birthday, and fully conscious of my world. I remember us walking into Foot Locker and looking over the shoes together. Everything felt normal; it's what we always did. I saw a pair of Reeboks that were popular at the time and said, "Dad, I want these," fully expecting him to buy them. There was no question. Yet he turned to me and said, "No." He never told me no. No? But that wasn't it, he continued, "I'm not going to always be around to get you stuff, Slugg. Understand? I might not always be able to get you what you want."

That was it. He continued shopping as if nothing had happened. Unconsciously, my father had responded in a way that was meant to prepare me for what was to come.

The Fall

I n 1985, by the time I was five years old, the Hanover I had grown to love was forever changed. Eventually those long lines on Hanover created a buzz loud enough for federal agents to hear. The two names they heard the loudest were Cornell Jones and Tony Lewis. So the local police and the F.B.I. teamed up to shut down the drug business on Hanover. Cornell was arrested on drug conspiracy charges after meeting with a government informant. He took a plea deal and went to prison on a nine- to twenty-seven-year sentence. Sometimes, I wish my father had gotten caught then too. But he didn't. He continued to run the operation on Hanover, briefly thwarting the authorities' efforts at shutting it down, until they took to occupying the neighborhood.

I remember the big blue and white police trailer with towering floodlights atop it. It sat on the block for many months as if Hanover was a construction site and there was a place needed for the developers and foreman to meet any time of day. Its presence, and the authorities housed inside twenty-four hours a day, eliminated my father's operation on Hanover permanently. All illegal activity on the block ceased. Quickly all the men and women who used to gather on Hanover found other places in the city to do their business, and so did all the people who came along with them. Overnight, the block that used to be teeming with life, that used to feel like an adventurous place to me, became like a ghost town.

Though they may not have had a full understanding about the positive effects of true community policing, I believe the police officers that occupied that trailer understood the importance to some degree. It's hard to say, as I was too small to read them, but I do remember them passing out hot chocolate to the children on the block. Perhaps it was only procedural, but it seemed like an effort to somewhat endear themselves to the community, or to soften the image of the monolith and the men that flashed blinding lights on us throughout the night. I never had a cup of cocoa. I had no need or desire for one. I drank many cups of hot chocolate at home, prepared any time I wanted by my mother. She'd pour the flowing goodness into colorful mugs embossed with cartoon characters on them.

My cousin Rico doesn't remember having a cup, either, though his experience was far different from mine. He *wanted* a cup. In that little two-bedroom apartment he sat and thought, fought with himself, over whether he should accept a cup of hot chocolate from the police trailer or not. He wanted a cup but worried that someone would tell on him. Would someone say, "Yep, I saw Rico take a cup"? These were his thoughts, a child pondering betrayal or a sweet, warm cocoa in his stomach. He chose loyalty. He stayed away from the trailer when other children didn't.

Though plenty of attention was paid to him, my father never

sought it. He didn't like the spotlight. In all that he had and did, he was trying to fill the hole inside of him. There's a great emptiness that comes with the way my father was raised. Growing up in the ghetto and coming from a broken home often does one of two things: either it reduces the spirit to submission, a dead calm within the chaos, a sad acceptance of lack and dysfunction, or it inspires wild and outlandish fantasies to acquire feel-good things. The cocaine explosion in the U.S. allowed my father to make his dreams a reality. In the hood, many dream of money, fancy cars, and stylish clothes. My father fell in line with that norm, but he also deviated from it by being a family man. As a boy, he dreamed of leaving the ghetto and raising a happy, prosperous family. Selling cocaine was the path he saw to help him do that. As much as he had a passion for fancy things, it paled in comparison to his fidelity and love for me.

When Hanover got shut down, my father eventually set up his own operation out of a house on 1st and Bates Street NW, which is only a few blocks from Hanover. Around the same time, I started to see Rayful Edmond III. He wasn't around at all in the early years. I just remember him being there all of a sudden. At the time, I viewed Rayful like a fun uncle. I even used to address him as Uncle Ray. There was something about him that made you want to like him. I think that's one of the reasons my father eventually warmed to him. He seemed to take life lightly, always joking around and pulling practical jokes. I remember him always smiling. He'd smile at me and say, "Here you go,

Slugg," and hand me a one-hundred-dollar bill.

Unlike my father, Rayful enjoyed the spotlight; he basked in it. He was tall and slim but had an athletic build. He glided when he walked, and his smile was bright enough to light up the darkest room. He and my father would be driving the same car side by side, but you'd see Rayful first.

It was common for my dad and Rayful to hang around each other's places of business. I never saw my father handle any drugs and was never around any drugs when I was with him. However, I was accustomed to seeing money. Once our basement flooded in Maryland, and some money that my father had in a safe hidden in the basement floor got soaked. I remember watching him as he laid out tens of thousands of dollars to dry. Sometimes I'd also be around them when my father and his men counted garbage bags of money. When I had learned to count, to occupy me, sometimes my dad would have me count the ones. I remember taking the job seriously, counting in piles of ten and stacking them opposite of each other to keep track.

One day when we were at the house on 1st and Bates, Rayful came through. As usual, there were a lot people hanging out in the front of the house. I can't remember who started it, but eventually a crap game broke out between Rayful and one of my dad's men named Fila Rob. My dad didn't participate, but it wasn't because he didn't gamble. He just didn't gamble anymore on the street; he preferred gambling in crap joints or in Las Vegas or Atlantic City. Rayful wouldn't normally gamble on the street, either, but at that moment he just wanted to have fun. Normally my father and Rayful would only bet with other hustlers or major gamblers that had "real" money—otherwise, to them, it was pointless.

The word went out quickly in the neighborhood that Rayful was gambling. In no time, a very large crowd of people surrounded the crap game. Rayful eventually won and beat Rob for about ten thousand dollars. Now here's the difference: had my dad been in that situation, he would have pocketed the ten thousand dollars and given it to someone in need, or he might even have given it back to Rob. Rayful took the stack of money and threw it in the air. Immediately, people from the neighborhood rushed in, going to their knees and scrambling to pick up as much as they could. I looked at Rayful. He was admiring the scene with a smile on his face. Then I looked at my father. He just shook his head.

I can just imagine a child who was present that afternoon running home and telling his friends he got money on 1st Street when Rayful Edmond threw *thirty* thousand dollars in the air. The money, which he wouldn't have had otherwise, was proof of his story. And poof, the money goes from what it actually was, around ten thousand dollars, to an inflated sum. Myths are born out of these kinds of moments, stories passed around becoming more fantastic each time. Each time the story is told, the crowd and money become larger than what they were in the previous version, and eventually it grows into a tale about that time when Rayful was out gambling on 1st and Bates and threw *one hundred* thousand dollars in the air.

Of course, I also know what it's like to live inside that legend. By 1989, when I was eight, my father and his then-friend Rayful were major celebrities throughout D.C. At the time, and in the minds of many from those parts of the city, no names were more prominent locally or globally with the exception of a megastar like Michael Jackson. Kids knew more about Rayful than they did about Martin Luther King, Jr. It sounds like hyperbole, but for that time in D.C., it was true. My father and Rayful were looked upon as superstars. Today it's common, but back then people in the city didn't see young black men doing the things my father and Rayful did. In many ways, the handful of young men like them scattered across the country in the drug trade were the originators of the flashy style popularized today by hip-hop culture. Back then, rappers emulated them; they wanted to be like the big-time drug dealer, and they weren't the only ones. It is strange how the transmission of culture happens, how things are taken; characteristics once exclusive to a tiny subculture spread throughout the world and become commoditized. For me, it's stranger all the more because I know firsthand the real hardship that comes from living inside that world.

My father was famous, and by extension people wanted to make themselves known to me. They'd come up to me with a story about some kind of association to my father or something they had seen him do. Mind you, this wasn't just in our neighborhood, it happened all over the city. It's a strange thing at first, especially for a little boy, but I got used to it. I was little Tony Lewis. Still, I had to be careful. I had to be cautious of people approaching, the way they spoke or looked. I had to be aware of my surroundings at all times because at the height of my father's fame, the city had grown dangerous. My father was well liked and respected in most circles, but in that era kidnapping was a very real and constant threat for the big drug dealer's family. I can't imagine the stress this put on my mother, hearing of kidnappings and murders and knowing that she and her son were prime targets.

My mother's paranoia grew with my father's success. Our drive from Hanover to our house in Maryland would normally take around twenty minutes, but when the violence in D.C. spiked our trips began taking over an hour. My mother would take various elaborate routes home, turning onto small side streets, lefts and rights, stopping and looking in the rearview mirror then continuing to create a maze for our would-be followers. This became routine. At the time, I didn't say anything but I recognized the difference. I fully realized our routes had changed and we were returning home later and later, but as an eight year old I couldn't appreciate the magnitude of it all, and I certainly couldn't see those mysterious mechanisms inside my mother's mind. Looking back, it's hard to say if she was mistaken for doing it: the times and our status may have called for it. Still, while people were buzzing about what they saw my father or Rayful out doing, where they went shopping, where they went to eat, what they were driving, my mother was driving a different route home every day and slowly beginning to unravel.

I knew something was wrong when I paged my father and he didn't call me back. He would always return my calls. I had been paging him with our various special codes for years. I learned how to do it at a very young age, beginning at around four or five. I would page him repeatedly. The numbers in a way said, "Where are you? Come get me!" and eventually he would, but not that time. We knew something was wrong, but we didn't know what. At the time, my father and my mother were at their rockiest, so he wasn't spending nights at our house in Maryland anymore. He would still come get me, though, and we'd spend time together like we always did.

The last night I spent with my father, we stayed together at his apartment in Crystal City. The night's so very clear to me. I was nearly nine years old, but I think I also remember it so well because I've been over it in my mind countless times. He and I watched the National Geographic movies that we both loved. One was about grizzly bears, and the other was about great white sharks. He had this leather reclining chair that massaged you as you sat in it. You could control it on the arm. I loved that chair, and that's where I sat. We ate Frusen Glädjé butter pecan ice cream, watched those movies, and talked like we always did. I didn't have any clothes at his apartment, so in the morning I put on one of his shirts. We left the apartment, got some food, and headed to Hanover where my mother was waiting for us. She had Rambo with her. And that's it. That's the last free memory I have with my father. Someone on Hanover happened to take a picture of us on that day. I used to look at it often and think of all the times we spent together. I look so happy in it.

After a few days of me paging him repeatedly and us not hearing from him, our home phone began to ring, but every time my mother would answer it the person on the other end would hang up. My mother was worried, as there had been rumors swirling that my father and Rayful had been arrested. Then came the night where it was confirmed.

Between 1987 and 1988, the murder rate in D.C. nearly doubled. As a result, the Fox News affiliate for D.C., Fox Five, created a program called "City Under Siege." It was filmed on a set designed to look like a police vehicle on a gritty D.C. street. It came on each night at eleven and highlighted all the criminal activity from that night and previous nights. It was April 15, 1989, and my mother and I were watching the program, partly because we watched it anyway and partly because we were looking for some news of my father. On that night, we heard the report we were waiting for.

The program showed my father with his hands behind his back and in handcuffs being escorted into a police station. He was wearing stonewashed blue jeans and a grey crewneck Georgetown Hoyas sweatshirt with white high-top Reeboks. The image of him set in for a moment, and then my mother started panicking. Were the Feds coming to our house? She started gathering all the pictures she had of my dad and Rayful together and cutting them up. We had something like fifty thousand dollars in cash at the house, which, after she finished cutting up the pictures, she took to Uncle Boo's house for safekeeping. That money would have helped us in the transition, but all of it disappeared without us seeing a dime of it. It was gambled away. I don't know who was responsible, Boo or someone else in his family. Regardless, all the cash we had would soon be gone.

I was afraid and confused. My mother's paranoia jumped to levels much higher than it ever had been, and she cried non-stop. I just wanted her to stop crying. It would make me cry. When she saw that her crying was affecting me, she'd hug me and tell me that everything was going to be okay, but her behavior told me that wasn't true. The faces of my family members told me that wasn't true. Everyone, on both sides of the family, stopped smiling. I wanted them to smile again, to break out in laughter, but they didn't. Everyone just kept telling me it was going to be okay with those sad, gloomy faces. At St. Margaret's, Mrs. Robinson, the school's principal, called me into her office and told me that she had heard what had happened to my dad and that they would be there for me. My fourth-grade teacher, Mrs. Brown, pulled me aside during class, looked me in my eyes, and told me that things were going to be all right, and I believed her. Aside from the gloomy faces, I believed everyone. My family told me that my dad would be home soon, and I believed that. I had very little understanding of the seriousness of the situation, and I wanted to believe that he would be coming home.

In D.C., my father's trial seemed to become the trial of the century. It was in the newspapers, on the radio, and on the television every day. I'd come home from school and see my dad's and Rayful's image splashed across the television screen. The trial received national coverage as well. Ted Koppel came to D.C. and held a town hall meeting about the effects crack had on our city and country, and Rayful was interviewed from prison by Diane Sawyer shortly after the trial ended.

There were a lot of things that happened in my father's case that were unprecedented for drugs cases in Washington D.C.: bulletproof glass in the courtroom, sequestered juries, the incarceration of him, Rayful, and a few other co-defendants in Marine Corps Base Quantico—to be flown by helicopter to the trial. The change that affected me most at the time was the judge's decision to grant no bail. My dad could not be home while he awaited the decision. Suddenly, visiting jail wasn't so much fun anymore.

Before my father went to jail, I was accustomed to prison visits. We would make it a family trip to go see my uncle Greg. To a little boy unaware of the gravity of the situation, it seemed like a good time. Everyone would be excited during the long drive, and when we arrived, Uncle Greg would be smiling, and my cousin, Nicki, his daughter, would be smiling. Perhaps seeing him there was different because Uncle Greg had been in and out of prison most of his life, and we had known him to be in prison all of our lives. Uncle Greg was already doing a sentence when I was born, so prison had been normalized for me from the start. Maybe Nicki wasn't as excited as I remember her being, or maybe her first time she wasn't excited. All I know is that my first time seeing my father in jail was one of the saddest days of my life.

He started out in D.C. Jail. I was used to USP-Lewisburg, where they had contact visits and vending machines. Contact visits mean just that—you can touch the person, hug the person; you're sitting in a visiting room together, and it feels more normal. But, in contrast, D.C. Jail felt like a terrible place. The receiving lines were long, and the staff was discourteous, disgruntled, and unprofessional, but all of that was nothing compared to the first sight of my dad. D.C. Jail was non-contact, so I had to talk to him through one of those fiberglass windows you see in the movies. What you don't get a sense of in the movies, though, is the smell of the place. That smell never goes away. Especially the phone; it had a lasting and appalling stench to it. Holding it against my face made me sick.

My dad was a high-profile case, so he was literally placed in a cage for the visit, which was different from the rest of the inmates. I sat down before the cloudy glass and the cage and watched him come in. He was wearing a bright-orange jumpsuit. In the holes of his Reeboks, where his shoestrings used to be, there was white cloth, which looked like pieces of bed sheets. His hands and feet were shackled, and he was shuffling toward me. Then he sat down on the other side of the glass. *But this is my dad. He had just been free, free to be with me and hug me. Now he's sitting in front of me like this? No. This is not him. This isn't us. This isn't how we are.*

46

He tried smiling at me, but I saw the stress, worry, and fatigue on his face. I had never seen that disoriented and confused look. But he tried to overcome it to talk to me and reassure me. I can't remember a word he said. I'm sure it was what most would think a loving parent would say to their child, but the shock of it all, the smell and the sight of him there like that, erased any lasting words. I think the initial shock was hard for him too. When you're in the life, you expect to go to prison at some point, but he didn't foresee the terms of his imprisonment—the no bail, and the cage.

When the first visit was over and I had to leave, I cried for an hour straight. In truth, that would be my reaction every time during that period. My mother and I would go see him on Tuesdays and Fridays every week at D.C. Jail. Eventually, once they got settled and the initial shock wore off, my father and Rayful received preferential treatment at the D.C. Jail. This is the stuff you see in the movies where the guys are eating steak and drinking champagne. That happened, but, for them, the retribution was swift. Soon Dad was transferred to Marine Corps Base Quantico. It was a little farther away and not as easy to go see him, though we still went frequently until he was placed in the custody of the Federal Bureau of Prisons.

On the day of the sentencing, my mother took me to Quantico. She waited outside in the car, and my father's girlfriend, Karen, accompanied me to my dad's cellblock. At Quantico, I had to visit my dad at his cell—him on one side of the bars, me on the other. It was a military facility, and they did not have standard prison accommodations. I'll never forget that last walk to see him there. Karen didn't walk with me. She'd later join me at his cell, but she knew I needed a moment alone with my father first. He happened to be in the last cell, so as I made my way down the long corridor, I'm walking past the grieving families of the other codefendants. Finally, I reached my dad and saw he was crying. It was the first time I had seen him cry, but I couldn't fully understand the gravity of the moment. I was a child, and I didn't know the terms of his sentence. But I understand it all perfectly well now. He was not crying about having to go to prison for his crimes. He was crying about his sentence: life without the possibility of parole.

In between the tears, he kept telling me I had to fight. "You have to be strong, son." Soon he would be sent across the country to a federal penitentiary in Lompoc, California, and the course of both his life and mine would be drastically altered. For all the comfort, security, and stability I experienced in my first nine years of life, the next nine would be the exact opposite.

My Mona Lisa

I couldn't have had a more loving or caring mother. She did all the big and little things that great moms do. She nourished and protected me, kept me clean and comfortable, and gave me all the attention I'd ever need. She educated and disciplined me, laying the foundation for my morality. For nine wonderful years, I had a balanced and secure upbringing. Then it all fell apart.

We lost our house in Maryland about a year after my father was arrested. My mother was a ball of emotions from the time my father was taken through the time we had to leave our home. In a second, she'd go from crying to raging. My father's arrest both upset and saddened her, but she was also hurt deeply by the shattering of their relationship and the new romance my father had with Karen.

When Mom wasn't focusing on my father or crying about him, her anger was directed toward dad's girlfriend. "That bitch, Karen..." became a phrase I got so accustomed to hearing during that time it still rings clearly in my head today. She'd be talking on the telephone to a friend or sometimes even to me, and she'd start into her tirade. "I saw that bitch, Karen, at the jail..." or "That bitch Karen thinks she..."

Karen had been one of my father's women for some time,

but his marriage proposal to her while he was at D.C. Jail exacerbated my mother's disgust toward her. I remember visiting my father at D.C. Jail and him asking me how I felt about him marrying Karen. What was I going to say? I said I didn't mind. It was the truth. Marriage was an abstract concept to me at the time and I was far more concerned with his incarceration. It was all so confusing. But to my mother, his proposal to Karen was the ultimate sign of betrayal. He was the only man she had ever loved.

Despite my father's other women, my mother had always been the one. She was special, the mother of his son and the only one to whom he had given a house and multiple cars. Her favorite car was the one she had received last. It was a white 190E Mercedes Benz. She loved that car. It distinguished her. Yet now Karen was going to take her place. Karen would be the most important woman in my father's life. My mother cried about his imprisonment more than she raged about his relationship with Karen, but the two events were closely linked. The matter with Karen just intensified an already highly charged situation. In addition to all the other emotions surrounding my father's situation, his relationship with Karen triggered some of my mother's deeply rooted insecurities.

My mother is very dark skinned; I get my color from her. I say this proudly, but unfortunately, our dark skin tone has always been a source of shame for my mother. The shame has a long historical connection reaching back to the transatlantic slave trade and a time in the western world where blacks were taught to hate who they were. White was right, and the lighter you were the more right you were. Sadly, this perception still exists in various places throughout the world today. The stigma burrowed into the consciousness of black people, causing many to hate themselves and the very distinct characteristics given to them by God. It created a subculture of hate within the black community, which continues today.

An incident with 2012 Summer Olympic gold medal gymnast Gabby Douglas comes to mind. After Douglas won the all-around gold, there was a ridiculous uproar in some circles of blacks about the coarseness of her hair. They said it didn't look good enough. They said it looked nappy. White people didn't get it. "Of course her hair might not look the best, she's a world-class athlete in competition!" some said in her defense. What they didn't understand was the lasting distinctions within black subculture, the culture that created brown paper bag tests and the term "good hair," all the comparisons to the supposed virtues of whiteness. Of course, many blacks also came to her defense as well. But her hair even becoming an issue demon-strates how that kind of self-hatred has persisted.

In D.C., there is a well-established history of a color line among blacks. In general, the lighter-skin blacks were granted more opportunity, which created a bourgeois class of blacks that looked down on the darker-skinned blacks. For a time, and still to some degree today, lighter-skinned black women were viewed within the black community as more beautiful and more desirable—women like Karen, who was a few shades lighter than my mother.

My mother was very fashionable. Long before she had access to the tens of thousands of dollars from my father's hustling, she was that way. Some people are born stylish regardless of their means. That was my mother. One's appearance mattered greatly to her, and in a sense her natural inclinations lined up perfectly with the material things she was able to acquire (clothes, shoes, jewelry) during those years where my father made a lot of money. Aside from the things she'd dress herself and me up in, she also took great care to make sure her hair, nails, and skin were perfect. It would take her hours to get prepared. Often she'd call me into her room and ask, "Do I look fat?" "Do these pants look right on me?" "Do these shoes go with this?" "What color should I wear?" "Is this too small?" "How does this shirt look?" I always did my best to answer her, but I don't know how much I helped. She had what she wanted to look like in her mind, and she always achieved it one way or another.

Yet along with her fashion sense and care about her appearance, she was also very self-consciousness about her weight. I never thought much about her asking me, "Do I look fat?" but looking back, some of her questions had deeper implications. I didn't know what to make of it then, but I can still hear reverberations of my mother retching. It sounds differently in my ears now, more ominous. It happened regularly; I'd hear her vomiting in the bathroom. I didn't know what to make of it then.

My mother's purging didn't have a direct effect on me, but I do wonder how it affected her long term. Through her, I now know that eating disorders are a common but well-cloaked disease. Unfortunately, we often take projections of ideals of beauty and misconstrue them as something we are supposed to be, what we are supposed to look like. But those projections are a show and often a sham. What's healthy and real is how you feel—feeling good about who you are and how you were made. We're all made differently, and that's the beauty of creation. We are all beautiful, and each has something wonderful to offer the world.

As a woman in her early to mid-twenties, my mother had no reason to think she was fat. She was a robust and curvy woman, but hardly fat. Yet she was looking at other women, the kind of women that started to be around my father—thinner women, less curvy women—and it made her feel bad about herself. I cannot and will not pretend to know what it was like for my mother or women in general who experience the same kind of thoughts or feelings. I know our society treats men differently when it comes to weight and health. There are stigmas for both genders, but the intensity and the pressure is far greater for women. But we should all strive to be content with the body types we've been given. The body is very much connected to the mind, which is very much connected to the spirit. In addition to all the outside pressures my mother faced—being from a fierce and unforgiving environment and, essentially, becoming a hustler's wife who was marked—I wonder how much my mother's insecurities led to what was to come next.

As a child, I didn't understand the seriousness of us losing our house in Maryland. I felt comfort in knowing that we had a home with my grandma on Hanover. The house on Hanover felt just as much like home as anywhere else. We were always there anyway, and that's where I wanted to be. Despite Hanover no longer being the bustling place of my early childhood, all of my friends were still there, and there were more in the surrounding area. As a pre-teen, I couldn't see that us moving permanently from Maryland to D.C. was like me at one moment going from standing in a domesticated pasture watching docile cattle with their heads down eating the plentiful grass to being stranded in a remote section of the Serengeti next to a wildebeest carcass and watching the big cats closing in. There's no escaping that. That kind of scenario was coming for me; I just couldn't see it because it wasn't our time to die yet, and my mother was crumbling before my eyes.

Our house wasn't in my father's name. Unless drug dealers have a legitimate business as a front, they don't put properties and cars and such in their names. He put our house in Grandma Lou's name, and when things started to go bad, Lou decided to sell the house. I still don't know the whole story, but we lost the house. Again, I wasn't affected by the idea of losing the house, but I was affected by my mother screaming at me, vilifying my father, "Yeah, you see this?" she'd say, "They putting us out. You love that motherfucker, but look how he got us." I didn't know what to believe. Nothing my dad ever did showed that he would not protect me and provide for me. The situation was new and strange, and it was about to become even more bizarre.

We should have moved to Hanover and stayed there. It was the first place we went, but my mother couldn't accept the truth of our situation. My father was gone, and all the money was gone, forever. Today I understand that, in any situation, a drastic lifestyle change is not easy to accept, especially when having lived many years in the previous lifestyle. My mother was born a princess, and because she was the baby of the Hinton family, she was treated like one. Then she was treated like a queen with all the gifts, privilege, and status symbols lavished upon her by my father. For ten years, she lived like that, never lifting a finger to work outside of caring for me and keeping her house together, both of which she enjoyed, and never having a material wish go unfulfilled. Then virtually overnight, that lifestyle was gone.

To care for my immediate basic needs, my mother became a school bus driver, but that job, its meager income, and us living in the house she grew up in couldn't satisfy her. So after living there for a few months, we moved into a nice two-bedroom apartment in New Carrollton, Maryland. From the start, we could not afford the place. I remember driving around with my mother in her Benz to places where she could catch up with hustlers like Ruffin, Fray, and Black Buster. We'd get out of the car and she'd greet them, talk a bit about my father, and ask for money. It didn't look like begging—my mother was too dignified for that posture, and my father's reputation with other hustlers brought respect and understanding. So for a while they gave my mother money, but ultimately she was asking something for nothing. There's little grace in that, and it could not last.

A part of my mother's clinging to the past was her wanting to do things for me, but it didn't affect me as it did her. I was too young to be covetous, and though the things were nice, I had not yet developed the lust that comes with materialism. She felt badly that she could no longer get those things for me. She felt badly that we couldn't go out to eat at the fancy restaurants together on a whim. So with the money she was able to scrape together, she tried to make up for what she perceived I was lacking. In her mind, I should lack for nothing nor want for nothing. Nothing should change in the way that she had raised me. I wish she could have separated the material stuff from the love. Her love was enough. Having her there as herself, attentive and doting and caring, with visions for a better life for me, working with me and dreaming with me, was enough.

About a year after my father was sent to prison, my mother and I were on our way to Hanover one evening when we stopped at a gas station in New Carrollton. After the car was fueled, my mother went to pay the attendant. I sat up front in the passenger seat bobbing my head and listening to music. When I heard someone opening the driver's side door, I turned and faced a man pointing a gun at my head. He screamed at me,

"Get the fuck out the car!" but I couldn't move. I stared down the dark hole of the revolver until I felt myself being yanked from the passenger seat and into my mother's arms. She had wings. I remember looking up and seeing the horrified look on her face and her holding me as we watched the man speed away in our car.

He took our car, my mother's precious 190E Benz, the last big material possession of our old life, but the incident did more than that. It confirmed my mother's worst fears and justified her paranoia. The screen in her that filtered reality and unreality was torn away. The carjacking broke her, and we were never the same.

Her condition wasn't apparent to me right away though. A week or so after the incident, we seemed to get back to us, to what had become our life with just the two of us. Then the first episode happened. It was nighttime and we were in our apartment in New Carrollton. I was in my room and she was in hers. Our rooms were side by side. Lying in my bed, I heard my mother talking to someone. It kind of sounded like a conversation she would have with one of her girlfriends. I had my own phone in my room so, slowly, I picked the receiver up and brought it to my ear to find out who she was talking to, but all I heard was the steady hum of the dial tone. I knew she was talking to *somebody*. I could hear her having a conversation. She was saying, "That bitch, Karen, set it up. She had that motherfucker come. I'm going to kill them motherfuckers if they fuck with my son. Everybody just jealous of me because I'm rich.

They all mad because I got money..."

I didn't know what to think, so I softly set the receiver back down on its base and walked to my mother's room. When I entered her room, I saw that she was talking to herself. Yet, something about it wasn't right. Something about it was different. I stood there and stared for a moment. I watched her go on talking as if someone else other than me was there to listen, as if someone other than me was responding to her—she was having a full-out conversation. Confused, I was hardly able to form words to speak.

When I composed myself, I said, "Ma, who are you talking to?"

She looked at me and responded, "Huh, boy, what you talking about?"

"Right now, Ma? Just then, who were you talking to?"

But the conversation went nowhere. It was my first time trying to speak rationally with her in that state, and I was taken aback. She flat out denied that she was talking to herself and made me feel like I was the one in the wrong. All out of sorts, I turned around and went back to my room.

Given my father's former life, no one knew if the carjacking was random or not. Regardless, my father was not there to protect us anymore. I'm not talking about in the way of the street. I'm talking about the way any good father would protect his family. A father's mere presence, the sound of his reassuring voice, is enough for the feeling of protection. At the time, my father was incarcerated on the other side of the country in

California. With the physical distance came the emotional distance. I had no one to talk to about what I had just experienced: the carjacking, my mother talking to herself, all we had endured, none of it. My dad was good for that. Both of my parents were. I could talk to them about anything, but as my mother's condition started to worsen, and I realized that I couldn't talk to her, I tried conveying what was happening to my father. He would call from prison, and when my mother wasn't close by, I'd describe her strange behavior. I'd give him examples of what she was doing in the best way I could, but he couldn't understand what I was talking about. For a while, the same thing happened with Grandma and Aunt Bonnie. I'd try to tell them that something was wrong, but they wouldn't listen or didn't understand. I see now that they didn't have any frame of reference for mental illness. With my mother having always been aggressive and being accustomed to a community that majored in all manner of strange behavior—a good bit of which I see now as mental illness—they just didn't understand until my mother's behavior became so erratic that her condition became self-evident.

But for the longest time I dealt with her deterioration alone. There were a couple of events not long after the carjacking that I think exacerbated her condition. There is a housing project that's a few blocks from Hanover named Sursum Corda. It was a place that would become extremely significant to me in my teenage years. Before then, I was very familiar with it because we had family and friends that lived there. I would go there with

Uncle Boo all the time. Uncle's Boo's oldest daughter, Uni, lived there, and not long after the carjacking, my mother went to visit with her. Somehow, during the visit my mother got into an altercation. She and another woman got into a fistfight, and while they were going at it, the woman picked up a pipe and struck my mother. My mom blocked it with her arm and wasn't hurt badly after the fight, but I think it added to her suspicion that someone was out to get us. And if that incident didn't convince her, me getting in a car accident and needing sixty stitches in my head certainly did.

I was going to Atlantic City with Uncle Boo's wife, Monica, and their children, Kim and Alan. We were on the New Jersey Turnpike and I was asleep, sitting in the back seat. A collision happened on my side of the car and, coincidentally, I was the only one injured. I woke up with blood soaking my shirt and coat. I remember Alan wiping the blood off my face and us sitting there waiting for the paramedics to arrive.

Once the doctors stitched me up and we left the hospital, Monica called my mother to tell her what happened, but she didn't bring me back home. Instead, we went on to New York City for a few days. When we finally arrived back in D.C. and my mother was told the story, she looked at all the stitches in my head and wouldn't accept that they came from an accident. She believed someone hit me in the head with a hammer. She truly thought there were people bent on harming us, and no one was exempt from her suspicion. With my family close but not understanding or in denial, and my father away not understanding either, my lonely internal life began.

When it was just my mother and me in our apartment, I bore the entire burden of her transition. Our solitary days there were filled with nonstop conversations she had with herself about who was trying to kill us and what she was going to do if they tried. She'd shout powerful outbursts at family members and women from Hanover that were not there, yet she would talk to them as if they were there. She'd argue with these illusionary figures. I knew and loved all of the people she fought with in her mind. The people were very real, but I was there and they were not. She and I were the only ones there. Not being able to stay silent on the matter, I began to challenge her or simply ask her whom she was talking about, and she'd lash out at me, "You don't know what the fuck you talking about. They trying to *kill* us, motherfucker." She'd yell at me saying, "Take that motherfucking gray shirt off. If they see you in that they gonna kill you. You a stupid motherfucker." My mother always was a curser, and before she became ill she occasionally cursed at me, but I was never *motherfucker.* When she used to curse at me, even while disciplining me, it was in a loving way, if that makes sense. She never cursed at me with a throat filled with rage. Now there was so much rage. She didn't cry as much anymore—her rage had devoured her sadness.

After a certain point, I just stopped challenging my mother or asking her questions about the things she was doing. It went nowhere. It didn't take long for me to see that her behavior was completely irrational. Sometimes, she'd be close to her old self, loving me and cooking for me, but she never returned to the way she once was. Even at peace, she didn't look the same in the eyes.

My first visit to see my dad in California came around this time. It was 1992, and I was twelve years old. Karen, now my father's wife, accompanied me along with my cousin Rico. Despite my mother's bitterness toward Karen, she allowed me to go. Given all that had happened in those three years, that first trip to California was really emotional. I hadn't seen my father for two years at that point, which was significant. Before he was incarcerated, he had never been away from me for more than a couple of days. But the first time he went to prison he went away forever. I couldn't control my tears in his presence. I cried every day the three of us went to visit him during our stay in Lompoc. My father tried to comfort me, smiling and putting me on his knee and kissing me like he used to when he was home. But there was so much going on inside of me. Along with missing him deeply and trying to take in the specialness of being together again, I couldn't help but notice how he doted on Karen. I didn't know my father had a romantic side. The way he held Karen and cuddled with her in that prison visiting room, the way his eyes went soft, I had never seen him be like that with my mother. Mom was back in D.C., struggling, and here he was like this with this woman. The significance of his union with Karen and how it affected my mother became clearer to me in that moment, and I felt greatly offended. "Hold up," I thought,

"You never touched my mama that way..." No, he didn't. I knew that he and my mother loved each other, but I never saw that love demonstrated in the manner that I saw in that visiting room. In fact, I saw the opposite of that.

During the 1970s, when my father was in his early teens, he started hanging consistently with my mother's brother, Uncle Boo. He'd come home with Boo, spending time at Grandma's row house at 39 Hanover Place. My grandfather died in 1966, so I never had the chance to know him personally. He and Grandma, Jabella Hinton—who was twenty-two years his junior—had five children. At the time of his death, my uncle Alvin was eighteen, my aunt Bonnie was seventeen, my uncle Greg was thirteen, my uncle Boo, whose real name is Alan, was ten, and my mother Samone was five years old. Granddaddy Hinton was a man for his family and a big man on Hanover. He was born in Warrenton, Virginia, but had lived most of his life in D.C. My grandparents met in 1945 when my grandfather rode through my grandmother's neighborhood in a Buick. It was a beautiful summer day in that American age where just riding along on a summer day was romantic. The Buick was a convertible, and, of course, Granddaddy Hinton came through with the top down, driving slow and looking cool.

Grandma was eighteen at the time they began their courtship. A year later, in 1946, they would marry and move into the two-bedroom apartment that my grandfather had on Hanover. Not long after, they moved across the street into the row house at 39 Hanover Place. My grandfather was a guard for the D.C. Water Company, and he drove trucks for a construction company, but his true profession was that of a gambler. He hustled craps and played cards. He even turned their basement into a crap joint. It was a place where you could drink, eat, gamble, and have an all-around good time. During this period, my grandmother was mostly a homemaker, but she also worked at a bakery, boxing up cakes, pies, and doughnuts.

Wanting the best education for their children, my grandparents sent all of their kids to Catholic school, but when my grandfather died, it destabilized the family. My grandmother got a job with the Bureau of Engraving and Printing and did the best she could to maintain the family's quality of life, but times got rough for a single mom in the ghetto with five children. Young men get away from their mothers in the city. The oldest, my uncle Alvin, was drafted into the Vietnam War. Being much younger than him, Uncle Greg and Uncle Boo got drafted by the block.

In the seventies, at the time my father started coming around, Grandma had moved out of her house and into a house uptown with her boyfriend at the time. She left the house for Aunt Bonnie and her husband Kenny, who were in their mid- to late-twenties, Uncle Greg and Uncle Boo, who were in their early twenties, and my mother, who was a teenager. Grandma would pop in on the children at least once a week, especially to see after my mother, but the day-to-day affairs of the house were generally run by the older siblings. By this time, the

64

Hintons were like royalty on Hanover; my uncles were a part of the hierarchy that ran the block, and my mother benefited from their influence. Being the baby of the family, she was used to getting what she wanted. With Grandma's work and my uncles' illegal activities, there was plenty of money to go around. By taking one look at my mother, the family's social standing was evident because she always dressed the part, wearing the latest fashions to perfection.

As my father spent more time in and around the Hinton house, my parents started noticing each other. My mother was only a year older than my father, but given her sophistication she seemed like a grown woman to him. Their relationship began with my mother having my father go run errands for her. She'd give him some money and say, "Go to the store and get me a soda," and would pay him for his service as my uncles would. At the time, my father was still very poor, so he accepted all requests that would lead to putting some money in his pocket. The change he was allowed to keep from their big money dice games could feed him and his siblings for a week.

But it was about more than that with my mother. She was beautiful to him. As a young woman, my mother was curvy and full figured. Her dark skin was clear and smooth, her eyes dancing. Her smile has remained the same, big and bright with a gap in between her two front teeth. There wasn't much my father wouldn't have done for my mother then. Their way with each other played out for a while, him running to get things for her and her paying him, coolly dismissing him in front of her groups of admirers upon his return. But beneath the veneer, my mother was watching my father, watching him around the neighborhood, how he handled himself, how he carried himself, watching him interact and observe Uncle Boo, watching him and seeing his essence beyond his material circumstance. Through this, unbeknownst to my father, he captured my mother's attention. She started hugging him in front of her girlfriends and calling him her *little* boyfriend before sending him off on another errand. This continued until one day she called him to her bedroom to run an errand and the dynamics of their relationship changed.

My mother inherited the Hinton family aggressiveness, so when she and my father became romantic, he became hers. Going out with Uncle Boo all the time was no longer acceptable. She wanted him by her side, in her room, spending every night together. Of course, he couldn't do that. He was a young man pulled by the allure of the street, and it caused some friction between them, which eventually led to the volatility that I became accustomed to seeing.

My mother was the only person that could make my father lose his cool. In everyday circumstances, he was always even tempered, smooth, and ready with a smile in front of those he loved, but with my mother it was different. They argued all the time—on our family trips, at dinner, and especially at our house in Maryland. Being the only child, there were no distractions or filters to keep me away from their altercations; I saw and heard everything, and at the time, it seemed to me that the fights were my mother's fault. She would just start yelling at him and insulting him. She'd say things like, "I used to buy you drawers, you dirty motherfucker!" She'd put her hands on him, shove him, and punch him in the face, and after enough of that behavior, my father would hit her back. They'd fight, and I'd be there to comfort my mother when my father had had enough and stormed out of the house.

Sometimes when my father would come home from a long night hustling, I'd just want to be with him. I'd just want to have fun like we always did, but so often, especially as I got older, my mother would flare up. I'd see it coming and think, "No, Ma, please not today. Just leave him alone." But she couldn't; it just wasn't in her. I know today that most of her behavior stemmed from the betrayal and pain because of my father's involvement with other women. My mother knew many of the women, and sometimes it would be a girlfriend of hers. I remember being in one of my father's apartments and answering the phone and talking to one of my mother's friends. Picking up the phone, I recognized the voice on the other end and called her name out. Knowing that I was young, she kept her cool and just asked to speak with my father. I thought it was strange for her to be calling my father at his apartment, but I didn't have enough understanding to know what was going on. I reasoned that she might have been looking for my mother, but of course she wasn't. Years later, I'd recall those moments and see the volatility of my parents' relationship in a new light.

Eventually, my mother and I were evicted from the apartment in New Carrollton and went to live permanently with Grandma at the house on Hanover. When Mom's condition began to worsen there, Grandma started to understand what I had been experiencing. My mother's episodes and erratic behavior became so pronounced there was no escaping it.

One night I woke up with Mom at my bedside standing over me with a frightening look on her face. "Where my motherfucking son at?" she asked me. "You ain't him," she said, then proceeded to point out things about me that were not right, which made me not her son.

I'll never forget that moment. It was the deepest pain. I could take being cursed at because at least then she knew who I was. But to look at me and not see me, to see someone else and not Tony, that was too much. We argued in the moment. "Ma, it's me!" I yelled. "How could I not be your son?" But she didn't listen; she couldn't understand. After going back and forth for a bit, she just left my room. I was overwhelmed by grief, but when it happened a few more times, I grew afraid. I was scared that my once loving and caring mother might seriously harm me.

I told my father about the incidents over the telephone, and at that point I still don't think he understood—prison has a way of freezing people in time—but through the consistency of my reports, he knew something wasn't right. After telling him of the bedside episodes, he told me that I had to protect myself, so I started barricading myself in my room at night, moving the dresser in front of the bedroom door.

These weren't things that happened once a month or even once a week; they happened daily. Every day there was something, either a repeated behavior or something new. In the early days, up through my high school years, a lot of it was new. She went through a phase where she would vacuum the hallway walls upstairs at night. When Grandma couldn't take it anymore, she'd come out of her room. I'd hear Grandma come out, and I'd come out. Grandma would say, "Samone, what are you doing?" This wasn't one of the times where she felt threatened. To her, the walls were dirty. She saw all kinds of grime and bugs, but Grandma and I saw the walls as they were, clean. The vacuuming would lead to Grandma and Mom arguing, and eventually Mom would go back in her room, but she'd continue making noise in there all night. This kind of thing happened night after night. It kept me up for a while at first, but eventually, I learned to sleep through it.

Beginning in late elementary school, my mother's illness colored every part of my life, including my academics. One night, during a fight with Uncle Boo, she literally colored my elementary school uniform. I was in the eighth grade at St. Margaret's. Because of our closeness of age, Kim and Alan were like Rico and Antonio to me growing up. Being Uncle Boo's children and relatives on my mother's side, I continued to spend a lot of time with them after my father went to prison. On the day of the uniform incident, Kim and Alan were staying the night with us at Grandma's house. We were all sleeping when out of nowhere my mother starts harassing Kim, telling her she had to get up and leave. Immediately, I knew what was going on, but this was before the family truly understood there was something wrong. It actually took a few years before they started to understand that my mother wasn't just dealing poorly with her lifestyle change. The night with Kim did it; it opened their eyes.

As my mother continued to go off, cursing and telling Kim she had to go, I looked at my grandmother and saw her confusion. Grandma couldn't understand why my mom was antagonizing Kim. My mother had always been so sweet to her nieces and nephews, and Kim hadn't *done* anything, but all of a sudden Kim had to go? Due to the shock of the moment, I don't know if Grandma remembers the words my mother was saying—her reasons for not letting Kim sleep and trying to get her out of the house—but I do. She kept repeating this: "People saying I'm trying to molest her. I ain't trying to molest that girl. Nobody trying to molest nobody. They got to go the fuck home. They can't stay here..."

It was the middle of the night, but my mother was going on and on, relentlessly insisting that Kim and Alan leave, and Grandma didn't know what to do. She and my mother started arguing, and Grandma told Mom that she was the one that had to go. Kim didn't have to go anywhere. Still in a fit, my mother ordered me to come with her. "C'mon, get your shit. We getting the fuck out of here." I listened. It was a school night, so I had to gather my clothes for the next day, which included my uniform.

During my mother's episode, while her focus was on Grandma, Kim called Uncle Boo. None of us knew it though, and when my mother and I descended the stairs and prepared to exit through the vestibule, Uncle Boo met us at the door. Boo was built like an NFL defensive lineman except he was short. He kept an impeccably trimmed beard and wore his hair brushed backward. Right away, he started yelling at my mother. "What the fuck wrong with you, Mona? You lunchin'!" He was confused and angry and this, combined with my mother's episode, made for an explosive scene. We were having some work done downstairs, and there were a couple of cans of paint against the wall in the vestibule. Uncle Boo and my mother began fighting, and as I put myself in between them, my bag fell out of my hands to the floor. In the scuffle, the paint cans were knocked over, ruining all of my clothes.

Somehow, finally, I was able to break them up and we went in opposite directions—me and my mother outside and Uncle Boo inside. We were leaving. That was her plan. But where were we going to go? None of the people my mother called came for us, and I was standing outside on a school night covered in paint. One of our neighbors had a little chair out in the front of her house. I was so frustrated that I picked it up and threw it. Up until that point, I had not shown my anger, and I certainly hadn't acted aggressively in front of my mother. I had the highest respect for my mother (I still do), and I had always done exactly what she told me to do with little to no resistance. But in that moment, out in the cold and covered in paint, I decided that being the son I once was no longer made sense. I was no longer going to go along with the irrationality as though things were like they were before. I would never again find myself outside for hours waiting for no one to pick us up, listening to my mother cursing and talking about who was trying to kill us. There was much about my mother's condition that I could do nothing about, but there came certain situations, like this one, where I could take a stand. I could say, "No, Ma, I'm not going."

After a few hours, Grandma eventually let us back in, and from that point on, I found myself comforting her and trying to protect her with regard to my mother. I didn't want her to have to bear the shock of it alone; no, she wouldn't go through what I had gone through. So, suppressing my own feelings even deeper, I was there for Grandma. Still, in so many ways, after my mother became ill, my family was there for me. I don't know where I'd be without them.

1st-and-O

With my father in the penitentiary and my mother suffering from mental illness, on the surface my family looked a lot like my friends' families. There was a single parent leading the home, my grandmother, with aunts and uncles passing through its doors possessing criminal records and a knack for getting by on street knowledge. But despite the surface characteristics of our home, my family was primarily governed by loving one another. Ultimately, the commonality that bound them to my life was that each of them was concerned with my wellbeing. They each took a vested interest in our family's legacy and poured whatever they had into the children, allowing me to grow up with security and confidence, imbibing lessons I'd find invaluable later in life.

My grandmother deserves much of the credit. With me at every step, Grandma went from being a grandmother in the traditional American way, sporadically doting, guiding, and spoiling, with only a small measure of responsibility for my life, to having virtually full responsibility for me. Her new role started as soon as my father went to prison. At the time, my mother was still able to work. Her job as a school bus driver began very early, so she was unable to take me to school. Grandma, who was some sixty years of age then, had been working for the Bureau of Engraving and Printing for three decades and was very close to retirement. She worked the night shift, and almost every day directly after work, she'd come pick me up from home to take me to school. On those mornings, I remember her being pleasant and calm, smiling warmly and hugging me when she arrived. We'd get in her Lincoln Town Car and be off. Grandma would be very tired. Often, we'd be driving along and come to a red light, and she'd fall asleep waiting for the light to change. When the light did change, I'd say ever so softly, "Grandma, the light's green." Waking up, she'd turn to me with smiling eyes looking through the dark glasses I had grown so familiar with, and then face the road to continue our journey.

When Grandma wasn't able, Uncle Alvin, whom we call Doc, would pick me up and take me to school. There were times where I didn't have lunch money, and Doc would deliver a meal to me at school. Doc always wore a baseball cap and a salt and pepper goatee that was unkempt. His legs bowed slightly when he walked like grandma. When I was growing up, Doc was mean. His glare was intense and piercing, and nobody in the family messed with him except me. I don't know what it was— perhaps because I had become accustomed to being around so many different kinds of people as a boy and had seen so much—but Doc's explosive rants and his scowl didn't affect me like they did everyone else. I'd smile and laugh at him. We had a unique relationship in that way because he didn't respond to me as he would others. He'd still curse me out, but it'd be with a smile hiding behind his scowl. "Don't mess with me, Slugg…" he'd say. So those times he brought me lunch to school he'd always curse me out and promise that I'd have nothing but the crumbs off my classmates' plates before faithfully showing up with something good to eat, but still wearing his scowl.

Doc's home was close to St. Margaret's school, so it became a natural stopover for me. Often Doc wouldn't be there, but I'd hang out with my cousins Kevin and Don or just be there by myself. I never had a key to Doc's house, so when no one was home, I'd have to climb through an open window. Doc had a pit bull named Rocky who fiercely guarded the house. I'd come through the window, and when Rocky would hear he'd start growling menacingly. But when he'd round the corner and see me coming through the window, he turned into a puppy dog. When Doc came home and found I had come through the window again, he'd be scowling and cursing me out, but he couldn't stay mad at me long. How else was I supposed to get in the house?

Doc's scowl could be attributed to his natural personality, but also to the things he saw as a soldier in the Vietnam War. One night, when I was around thirteen, we were all at Uncle Boo's crap joint in Cheverly, Maryland, watching the Vietnam War movie *Hamburger Hill* on VHS. The movie was based on the true events of a battle that took place on the Ap Bia Mountain in South Vietnam. Some of the guys in the crap joint were watching the movie and had an occasional comment here and there. No one asked Doc any questions even though he was some authority on the Vietnam War. Of course, all of us knew he went and made the connection, but we didn't really look at him through that lens. Plus, Doc didn't talk about it much, so it felt like we were all watching the movie as equals experiencing it from the same vantage point. But then there came a point in the movie when the American soldiers began to suffer heavy casualties, and out of nowhere Doc yelled, "They should've never sent those boys there!" When I turned to look at him, I saw he was almost in tears. His familiar scowl was shaded by a type of angry emotional response I had never seen in him.

The only other time I had seen him get that emotional was a few years before, after my father's conviction. While everyone in the family kept telling me things were going to be okay and putting on the face, Doc was the first to let me know, indirectly, that things weren't okay. Around that time, he and I were in his car together when the news of my father's sentencing came on the radio. What they were saying and the terms were unclear to me, but Doc started crying. There he was just breaking down in front of me. Doc didn't say it, but I knew it had to do with my father's sentence. I could feel it. But Doc's emotional response watching *Hamburger Hill* was different. I recognized the pain and emotional trauma that the Vietnam War had caused him, and the moment stayed with me. I came to learn that the veterans of the Vietnam War taught the medical world and the general public much about the ill effects that modern warfare, and warfare in general, had on the psyches of its soldiers. Before reading about it in a book, however, I had already learned all that I needed to know seeing my uncle's face that night.

Seeing that Doc got emotional in the crap joint about his experiences in Vietnam was both remarkable and unremarkable. Remarkable because one wouldn't think the crap joint was a place to experience those kinds of intimate emotions. A lot of emotions were displayed in the crap joint, but very rarely if ever of the kind Doc showed that night. Yet, it was unremarkable because Doc was a gambler, and gambling spots were like his second home. So if a moment came over him, there was a good chance it would happen at a gambling spot. Doc preferred to gamble on the horses, but he was in the crap joints plenty enough.

From the age of eleven, I was going to crap joints with my uncles Boo and Doc. Doc used to pick me up from school, and we would go straight to Uncle Boo's place. All the players would be gambling in the main room, and I'd be off in another room doing my homework. But as soon as I was finished, I would come into the room and watch the crap game. I learned a lot in this environment. The spots would be filled with older men who had seen a lot of life. One day one of the well-known big money gamblers, Warren Jackson, pulled me aside when I emerged from the room having finished my homework. "Stay in them books," he said. "Keep studying your lessons. 'Cause I'm telling you, trying to get all I ever wanted, I lost all I ever needed."

Doc didn't play nearly as much as Uncle Boo. Boo had a real passion for it. But Doc would often cut the games, meaning he watched the dice and controlled the game. In the hood, the dice are played on the ground, but in the crap joint they are shot on a table, like a pool table, not all that different from the craps tables in Vegas or your local casino. The house got one dollar for every ten dollars you made. Doc was the guy to collect the house cut of your earnings.

Crap games are chaotic, but it's a controlled chaos. Games can be as small as having three or four participants to as large as forty people. One person shoots the dice and one person fades the dice, and everybody else is betting with or against the shooter. The shooter can also bet against anybody willing to bet him as long as he can cover the bet. The object is to throw a seven or an eleven on your first roll—which is a win—and not throw two, three, or twelve—which are losses. If you roll four, five, six, eight, nine, or ten on your first roll, then that's your "point." The goal is to roll your point number again before rolling seven. If you roll seven before rolling your point, you crap out, meaning you lose.

In the big games, forty-some-odd people yelling bets back and forth to each other might seem to be a recipe for disaster, but it works. The possibility of gaining money connects people in such a way that the bets synchronize. It's similar to the old trading floors on Wall Street. Communication that might seem like gibberish to the outsider is perfectly understood by some-one who's a part of that world. You might hear things like "$20 I shoot?" "$40 you miss." "Bet a $100 on the bar," "bet I six eight," "bet 10 and 10," "bet he hit," "bet you don't 9 to 5," "bet back," and "you got more gates than Lorton."

I knew the concept of craps by the age of six. I remember when Squirm, Uncle Boo and Dad's man, bet me because he thought I didn't know what I was doing. I was about seven years old, and I'm shooting the dice. I hit my point, yet he tried to take his money. Offended, I snatched the money out of his hand and tore it up because he was trying to cheat me. Naturally, we little guys emulated what we saw. I had my dad and Uncle Boo to pattern myself after.

In my era, we didn't have the huge money games where hundreds of thousands were being gambled, but there were still some thousands to be won. And when you are a teenager, the prospect of having a nice bankroll is alluring. I had what we call a "good hand," meaning that I could throw and hit my numbers or points. My favorite number to catch was nine. I would roll the dice and say "45s and Glocks" or "What number did Jordan wear when he came back?" Then I'd roll the dice.

Hitting your point is exhilarating; there are not many rushes that feel better, but crapping out makes you feel just the opposite. It's a game of extreme highs and lows. Uncle Boo taught me to play the odds. The dice are going to miss more than they make, so it was best to bet against the dice. This meant even when your man is shooting. This philosophy was hard for me. I'd feel disloyal if I bet against Shakey or later my man PT. Still, Uncle Kenny, who was Aunt Bonnie's husband, taught me to never bet with emotion.

Next to Grandma, Aunt Bonnie was my other surrogate

mother. Bonnie was tall and heavyset. She wore her hair short and natural, which went perfectly with her round face. She had a radiant smile and a booming voice and laugh to go with it. A year younger than Doc, Bonnie's the second oldest of my mother's siblings. Except for Doc, all of my mother's siblings dropped out of high school. I think my grandfather's passing had a lot to do with that. He was very important for stability in their lives. As young people, Bonnie, Boo, and Gregory were charged on the same bank robbery case. Bonnie was found guilty of aiding and abetting and did a year in federal prison. When she was released, she earned her GED and later participated in a program sponsored by President Lyndon Johnson, which would lead to her getting a job with the U.S. Department of Agriculture. She'd work there for the next thirty plus years.

Bonnie loved my mother, but growing up they seemed to have a love/hate relationship. They would always curse each other out and say hurtful things to each other. They seemed to compete for friends and bicker over the smallest issues. But with me, Bonnie's love was unwavering and unconditional, and that love strengthened when my mother and I needed her the most. She and Grandma stepped up big when my mother fell ill. They were a tag-team duo that helped to keep me in line and put a positive life into perspective. They'd bring the blurry uncertainties into focus for me. I never wanted to let them down.

Often, I would catch the subway from my elementary school in Maryland to Bonnie's job at the USDA and wait for her to get off. I would sit in her office and do my homework and talk to her coworkers. Growing up in a neighborhood where few had jobs, knowing that Aunt Bonnie and Grandma went to work every day was important, and being able to hang out at Aunt Bonnie's office all the time had a tremendous impact on me. How many children from the hood get to see, practically daily, an alternative path? Desks and cubicles, and people dressed up nice and speaking professionally, making a living and a difference in people's lives. The possibility and the feel of it stuck with me.

Bonnie and her husband Kenny taught me responsibility. Bonnie moved back to Hanover in the early 1990s, and she and Kenny stayed with us at Grandma's for several months before saving up enough money to buy one of the row homes on the block in 1993. They lived in 27 Hanover Place, and we lived in 39. I didn't have to do chores at Grandma's house, but Kenny and Bonnie would make me do them at their house. Bonnie used to say, "Y'all gon make that boy a damn bum!" Everything Bonnie says she yells. That's her natural speaking voice. She's also blunt and brutally honest. Kenny, who received about $350 a month in disability, would give me $40 a month from when I was thirteen until nineteen. He'd require that I do little tasks around the house like picking up behind their pit bull named G and taking the trash out. Most times Kenny and I would just talk about life and the streets. He was a retired street dude. A shotgun blast to the leg left him permanently disabled, so he walked with a pronounced limp.

Kenny's mother was one of Grandma's best friends, so he was like a son before he became her son-in-law. He was from Southeast but was around our neighborhood all the time. Being much older than my father and Uncles Greg and Boo, he'd tell me about our family's history. I loved hearing his stories about my father and my uncles as they were growing up. The talks helped me to gain a deeper understanding of the past and the events and circumstances that made the men in my family. One can only teach what he knows. Kenny knew about survival in the unforgiving city streets. Once, he had a conversation with me about how to kill a man and get away with it:

"Dress up or mask up," he said, "and always use a revolver. Preferably a snub-nosed .38; they don't jam. And go alone. You can't tell on yourself."

Yet, in addition to lessons on street knowledge, he'd always encourage me to do well in school. Kenny didn't know much about going to school, and he couldn't speak on the specifics. He certainly had no idea what it was like for me going to school, but he knew it was the right thing to do. Though he didn't have the opportunity, inside he knew getting a sound formal education was one of the great civilizers. I saw it in his eyes every time he reassured me. He wanted better for me. He didn't want me to kill a man. But still, coming up around Hanover, he wanted me to be equipped to survive. Yet, far more than that, Kenny and all of my family wanted me to thrive. They wanted me to do well in the world. To get an intellectual grasp on as much of it as I could. His lessons were a part of that, building blocks. He saw that I could handle the information and would do the right thing with it.

Sometimes, Kenny liked to shoot heroin. Later, when I started driving, I would take him to the dope strips in Lincoln Heights and 58th St. for him to cop. He never shot it in front of me, though, and neither he nor I ever mentioned any of this to Bonnie. Kenny's dichotomy—deep love for family and living a life of crime—typified the manner of all the men in my family. He and I had a special bond.

With my father incarcerated on the other side of the country, collecting father figures was important to me. In my generation, a crisis quietly arose in large segments of black American families. At some point, the fundamental structure and nature of many black families changed; every other household began to function at the total exclusion of men. Black fathers just were not there—not in the homes and not in their children's lives; they were gone as if taken away by some strange force.

In the recent past, the fatherless phenomenon was stranger still because only a few—both those with large platforms and those within the communities most affected—felt it necessary to discuss the issue. The single-most impactful issue plaguing black communities across the country was, relatively speaking, hushed.

Families aren't supposed to function with one parent. Children need a pair of loving parents. Parents don't necessarily have to love each other and don't have to live under the same roof, but, somehow, they must work together to give equal parts of love to their children.

Given prison, death, and abandonment, in my neighborhood the number of homes without a father was extremely close to a hundred percent. Worse yet, for a number of reasons, some similar to the father's absence, many of the mothers around Hanover didn't raise their children either. So raising the children was often left to the grandmothers, and thus the total break-down of the most fundamental unit in life was complete. These kinds of failing families came to shape thousands of neighbor-hoods across the country. They represented a significant portion of the fatherless state of black families and nearly all those who would flash across the screen of your local nightly news and the tens of thousands you don't see going to prison. These families and the conditions of the community, both in substance and in spirit, created a pipeline to prison and a generation so lost and deadly that hope seemed futile.

My father's brother, Uncle Tyrone, was murdered when I was about thirteen years old. Ty was the first to be killed in our family, but I can't remember the exact date of his death. The early 1990s was a haze of loss for me. Back then, I was coping with the departure of my family while coming of age in the heart of carnage. War waged across the country. Washington, D.C., had the most deadly battlegrounds, and my backyard was a battlefield.

D.C. started gentrifying around the time my mother and I moved back in with Grandma permanently, and Hanover was hit hard. Million-dollar homes on our street were still twenty-something years away, but we watched as the initial stages of the movement forced every family on welfare off the block. Families I had known for years, like the Freemans and Dicks, scattered to other parts of the city. Hanover became a true ghost town then, far more so than when the police parked a trailer on the block. Now only a few homes were occupied on the entire block, and even people who owned their homes started to sell. Some, whose homes were paid off and had been in their family for generations, no longer paid their property taxes. Liens were put on their homes, and they were subsequently sold at auction.

Hanover is only blocks from downtown D.C., yet given its reputation, buyers stayed away. For years, the property values remained extremely low, and our once lively block remained barren. When I was an adolescent, this left a serious void for me regarding people to hang out with. Due to my father's reputation and riding around the entire city with Uncle Boo, I was friendly with everyone in the area surrounding Hanover. Still, I was much closer with the people on Hanover. Now that they were gone, I began to venture through the alley on O Street to hang with new friends. Lil' Dennis lived near the intersection of 1st Street and O Street, a corner where a bunch of the neighborhood boys would meet and form the 1st and O crew.

The intersection of 1st and O is close to Dunbar High School. Behind the high school, there's a large stretch of concrete where the boys from 1st and O played football. They called the playing surface "The White" because of the lightness of the concrete. The White had a large brick wall on one side and a high chain-link fence at the other. It was their arena, their field, and very soon it would become mine. We played gladiator ball on The White—full contact, no pads, no helmets, crashing into each other and falling to the pavement as though it were a soft bed of grass beneath us. Games on The White were proving grounds. Coming from Hanover, I was untested, the outsider, and upon my first invitation to The White no one knew what to expect from me. How tough were you? In our neighborhood, where we were rising to understand hardship and untimely death, to stare both in the face without blinking, toughness meant everything. Along with us pre-teens and teenagers, grown men occasionally played on The White, but they wouldn't hold back. They'd hit you with the full force of their power, slamming you to the concrete, and would talk shit after the blow to add insult to injury.

I was pudgy as a child. My man Scoop called me Fats even though he was just as pudgy as I was, except he was taller. Everyone also knew, on some level, that I was Tony Lewis's son, and with that came the suggestion of privilege. I put all the speculation to rest once I stepped foot on The White for the first time. Fearlessly, I tore into my opponents without any regard for my body and wellbeing. I tried to hit the hell out of whoever had the ball or whoever was in my way getting to the ball. Feeling the crunch of the concrete beneath me for the first time, I popped right up and continued popping up all game, no matter how hard the blow I was given or dealt. For a fat boy, I was also deceptively fast. I had good hands and quick feet, so as an offensive player I also gained respect. My performance on The White that first game earned me total respect, and it initiated me into the 1st and O crew.

My friend Jerry and I played football together at the number two Boys and Girls club, even though he was four years older than me. He introduced me to his brothers James and Jerome. I knew Tim and Shakey because we shared a family member (Uncle Gregory's daughter Shawnette was their first cousin). I was introduced to Fat Man and Zuchi. I already knew LT. He was from Hanover but had moved to O Street. Then my man Lil' Calvin (aka Head) from N Street joined the crew. Then there were the Johnsons: Marcha, Stinka, and Bobby. Their fathers and uncles also used to hustle around Hanover, so we grew close.

The Johnsons had three older cousins in the crew who we also looked up to: Big Dennis, Poochie, and Dolley Joe. We all came of age during D.C.'s crack era, and along with Uncle Ty, Big Dennis and Poochie were the first casualties to have a significant impact on me. All along I had been hearing about murder— bodies. As boys, death surrounded us, but to have full consciousness of it, to have known the deceased intimately, was different. Big Dennis was killed in a neighborhood called Florida Park. Poochie was shot and spared death only to be paralyzed from the neck down.

In 1980, my father was a young drug dealer when Richard Pryor set himself on fire. After details of the incident spread, there was a great spike in cocaine sales. Amazingly, people wanted to get high like Richard. At the time, many blacks believed powder cocaine to be the rich white man's drug. Limited to tiny subcultures across the country, most notably in California, freebasing was even lesser well known. Yet Pryor's low point became unbelievably effective advertising for freebasing coke, especially for blacks.

The crack epidemic hit Washington, D.C., more severely than any other city in America. One only has to compare D.C.'s arrest, murder, unemployment, and infant mortality rates from 1986 to 1996 to other major American cities in the same categories. I'm no statistician, but I've studied the numbers to get a better understanding of my history and my city's history. Beyond that, what other major American city captured the nation's attention *twice* due to singular figures and their cocaine usage? In addition to Len Bias, who was from Landover, Maryland, and attended the University of Maryland, both places less than twenty minutes away from D.C., former D.C. Mayor Marion Barry made national headlines when federal agents caught and filmed him smoking crack. Crack turned D.C. into the murder capital of the United States.

Though talked about a lot, the impact the crack epidemic had on the nameless is still underappreciated. The crack epidemic devastated values and left behind three generations of disturbed people: those who were addicted, the dependents of the addicted who witnessed the transition, and those who were birthed into its chaos.

In my neighborhood, crack created a culture of amorality, if not in body then certainly in mind and spirit. It removed mothers from already fatherless homes and destroyed the bedrock of the family. I've seen it with my own eyes. I've seen mothers prostitute themselves and pimp their daughters for hits of crack. As a matter of fact, the mother of my once good friend, Fat Man, made herself available to older guys in the crew. Some of their first sexual experiences were with Fat Man's mother. Fat Man not only knew about it, but he had to endure ridicule from certain members of our crew. Most of the crews' mothers were addicted to crack, so the ridicule would only go so far. Still, Fat Man stood out because his mother was one of the worst off.

Colloquially, many know crack cocaine addicts as crackheads. It's a word that's stuck in popular culture and often is used jocularly, but in my neighborhood, we called them pipe heads. Once you became a pipe head, you were looked at as non-human. You were close to human, but not quite. You knew the person had to have some humanity in them because they were someone's relative, someone's mother or father, uncle or aunt. But if the person was heavily addicted for too long, you seemed to forget they were human. Sadly, Uncle Ty fell into this category. I never looked at him as non-human. He was my uncle, but I'd be disingenuous if I said other people didn't look at him that way.

Uncle Ty would come around the neighborhood to check on me after my father went to prison. He'd borrow money from me. I'd be at a crap game shooting dice, and he'd ask me for five dollars. Mind you, I was around eleven or twelve years old at the time. I'd look up from my game, give Uncle Ty a twenty-dollar bill, and tell him to go to the store and bring me my change. He wouldn't come back. I wouldn't see him again for a week or two, and when I did see him he certainly wouldn't have my money. He'd be asking me for money again. But I didn't mind—he was my uncle.

Ty was getting high off other drugs before crack, but like tens of thousands of others, crack overpowered him. Before then, I remember him as a handsome young man who was always well groomed. Ty was light skinned and had wavy hair that he'd brush all the time. He also had a very short temper and would always be arguing and fighting someone. He was known to be a fierce and adept fighter who wasn't afraid of anyone. These parts of his nature persisted when he was heavily addicted to crack. It made him bold enough to rob some local dealers' stashes for drugs, and when the dealers eventually caught Ty, they killed him.

I've seen monstrous acts done to addicts for sheer amusement. I've seen them shot to see if a newly acquired gun worked correctly. I've seen them beaten, stabbed, and sexually humiliated in order to make other people laugh. Often, addicts would voluntarily put themselves in life-threatening and humiliating situations just for the possibility of scoring crack. The person inflicting the harm would feel justified because, again, the pipe head wasn't human. He or she wasn't a real person in the eyes of the abuser. The system of beliefs of that time was just awful. Because of the things I saw done to addicts when I was a child, I better understand the sick rationalizations of those who did horrific things to blacks when we were widely considered less than human.

Crack took neighborhoods that were already troubled and quickly eroded the last reserves of innocence. It took teenage boys who were wholly unprepared and made them the head of the household. It had us thinking we were men when we were the farthest thing from being a man. We thought power, money, and the ability to have sex with a woman made you a man. Most people can't imagine being twelve, thirteen, or fourteen and being offered sex by a grown woman, by women often twice our age. I remember an addict and grown woman named Natalie gave the entire crew gonorrhea. Though I was far from innocent, I wasn't in the number. I was propositioned daily by addicts in the neighborhood, but I wasn't going for that move. One of the women noticed my constant abstention and used to say to me, "You gon give me that dick one day," but I never did. I was after the challenge, young girls our age who still held some virtue, but crack changed the normal relationship dynamics for most of our neighborhood. Teenage pregnancy was at an all-time high in D.C. For example, my man Lil' Dennis had two kids at sixteen. Stinka had three kids by the time he was fifteen.

I'm a member of a furious generation—a generation of

young men who had their mothers taken away from them, a generation who never knew their fathers or had their fathers taken away, a starving generation, starving for love, nourishment, and attention. As infants, someone protected us; we wouldn't be here had they not, but how well we were protected is up for debate, and after infancy this protection was quickly removed. We saw *everything* and we were frequently in danger. Too often we were harmed in our own homes, and when we took to the street, we were harmed there too. We came up as targets, hurt, scarred, and angry over the abuse. In our world, something harmful—obvious or inconspicuous—was always skulking, ready to strike. So when we got old enough and strong enough to strike back, we did so with a vengeance. Others had to pay for whomever or whatever had harmed us. No one valued our lives, so why should we value anyone else's? This was unspoken, but deep down it screamed inside of us. We howled on the inside "I wish you would. I wish you would step to me. I wish a motherfucker would." Young men are already wired to fight—not all, but many. You throw that makeup into our situation, and there's little need for provocation. Existing was provocation enough.

In one way or another, every young man in my neighborhood smoldered with this feeling. So toughness and the deep need for one's power to be respected became law. I was born into respect and earned it. All the old heads in the neighborhood respected me because I was little Tony Lewis. By the time I reached my early teens, my cousins Rico and Antonio had established themselves as hardened street dudes. They were a part of the well-respected LeDroit Park crew, but they were from Hanover and would still come around. Guys they used to hang with—my big homies: Big Mix, Moe Man, Drew, Alan, Earl, Tim-Tim, Fat Mike, MG, and Rickey—would all sometimes hang with me as if I were Rico and Antonio. My peers looked up to me because of that. They also looked up to me because I dressed nice. Nice clothes represented style and the appearance that one was fresh, clean, and unaffected. Wearing the latest name brands showed that you were on top of things and in no way soured or affected by our circumstance. Of course, this wasn't true.

Mainly, I was respected by my peers not because of my legacy but because of the reputation I had built for myself. I was tough, street smart, and quick to fight. Like my Uncle Ty, I had a short temper. I too didn't need any provocation. I harbored hurt and willingly, sometimes eagerly, hurt others in response to what I was feeling.

We would play this violent game called hitting off the top. Essentially, we preyed on unsuspecting men, young and old, who dared to walk our block. Hitting off the top meant punching some person in the face and seeing if you could drop them with one punch, or better still, knock them out. If you didn't knock them out, then the entire crew would follow up and savagely beat the person. This was all for having the audacity to walk up the side of the street where we all stood, for walking past us and thinking there wouldn't be a cost. Jerry, who was a few years older, and I were known as power punchers. Smashing our fists into the faces and bodies of random people passing by was fun to us, and I'd always be one of the first to swing.

What's strange, though, is even then I'd bring things that I was learning to share with the crew. By my sophomore year in high school, virtually all of 1st and O had dropped out of school. We had guys that had dropped out of junior high. I don't know if unconsciously this had some kind of effect on me, knowing they weren't in school, but I've always been one to share what I knew if I found it to be interesting or thought it could be helpful—but I never lectured, I spoke. I spoke as if we were talking about something that had happened around our way. For me, it's never been about the soapbox or the lectern. It's all about connection, reaching people, looking in their eyes and knowing something I'm saying is resonating. One day when we were posted for a game of off the top, I distinctly remember relating what I had learned about Marco Polo to the crew. Why Marco Polo? I don't know. We were young, late elementary school-aged kids, but the memory stands out. I'm facing the street and telling of Polo's exploits when I spot a mark. I remember stopping my story, saying quietly, "We got one..." and launching myself from the crowd to punch the guy in the face. That's about where the memory loses clarity. I can't say whether he fell from that particular blow or how the beating went. Unfortunately, we did it so much that my talking about Marco Polo was the only thing that distinguished it from all the other times.

When I would swing first, and even when I didn't, I would

screen who was to be hit. It couldn't be someone who didn't exude strength. It couldn't be someone who looked like he stayed in the house and had some semblance of fear already in his step. This didn't make the behavior any better, but now looking back I think it was indicative of the kind of moral compass that I lived by. This understated sense of morality would continue to grow in me as I aged. Later on, it often left me deeply conflicted. It also sometimes left me more vulnerable than I should have been. Where I'm from, in the midst of the drama, there's no time to think.

Needless to say, we developed a reputation for playing this game, and dudes our age from other hoods knew it. People wouldn't even walk on the side of the street where we were posted anymore. We had established something of our own, something secure. We were not to be messed with. We were to be feared, and in that, we were to be respected.

We would continue to further our reputation as a hood to be respected, and I was at the center. When any of them would get into a rumble, they would call on me and I would be there to fight or squash the situation because a lot of times I knew the other parties involved. I carried myself like an older guy; I had watched the greats. I had it and I knew it. I would mimic my father and Uncle Boo. I led and always supported my team. I shared everything with them, including my home. When Cornell Jones was released from prison, he bought me the original Sony PlayStation, and everyone would come over to play it. Before they started hustling and had money of their own, my friends would all wear my clothes and Grandma would feed them. They needed me and I needed them. They were my brothers.

By the time I was thirteen, most everyone from 1st and O had jumped off the porch. They started stealing cars for fun and joy riding, selling fake crack, which we called "demos," to actually selling real crack for someone, to copping cocaine themselves, cooking it, cutting it, bagging it, and hustling for themselves. Once this cycle started, there was no turning back.

Murder Capital

Gonzaga is an all-boys Jesuit school and one of Washington, D.C.'s top academic high schools. Its admissions process is highly competitive, and its tuition is expensive. At the end of junior high, I had the grades to get in, but with my father gone and my mother on the verge of losing her bus-driving job due to her illness, there was no way that we could afford it. Still, my mother insisted that I apply.

This was a couple of years after the carjacking and all the incidents in our apartment in New Carrollton. We were back on Hanover living with Grandma. At the time, my mother's mind had not wholly betrayed her. There were more lucid periods back in those days, so I cannot attribute the irrationality of applying to a school we could not afford to her illness. No, her insistence came from another place. It came from my childhood, from the dreams she had for me being among the best and brightest students and taking what I learned there to help transcend my circumstance.

But for me it wasn't as simple as going to a great high school, which opens the door to going to a great college, which opens the door to a great career. It's really never that simple from anyone's perspective, but least of all mine. I couldn't appreciate the things I learned at Gonzaga until I was able to wrest myself from the deadly grip of my environment.

There was a guy named Meaty who had a similar background to mine. He lived in the Sursum Corda housing projects, and like me attended Gonzaga with the help of scholarships, but Meaty didn't go on to the good college or get the good career. A few years after high school, Meaty was charged with murder and is now serving time in prison. So, no, it's not as simple as where you go to school. There is no doubt that being properly educated helps tremendously in the loosening and freeing from abject poverty and a whole host of pathologies, yet education and having the ability to attend places of higher education alone is not enough.

Every year, Gonzaga sent home a directory of the families who attended the school and an alumni book that listed their professions. I remember looking through the directory and seeing husband and wife, mother and father, listed by the name of each student. Often there were titles attached to the names like congressman, general, professor, doctor, esquire, sometimes on both names. When I reached my place in the directory, there was only one name to represent me: Samone Hinton.

I didn't make it to any of the open house events leading up to my attending Gonzaga nor did I attend freshman orientation, making my first day stepping foot in Gonzaga the first day of school. I think it would have helped had I gone to some of those things, but my family didn't know or, if they knew, they didn't know of the importance of such things. My mother had handled my enrollment, but her condition was getting the best of her at the start of my freshman year. It was an achievement just getting me in the door on the first day. I don't know the exact cost of tuition then, but even when I attended Gonzaga cost thousands of dollars. My freshman year I received half my tuition cost in scholarship, but the rest we had to come up with. My mother had lost her job, and we had fallen behind on tuition payments, so by the end of my freshman year we owed a lot of money. The school wouldn't allow me to take my final exam unless we paid off the balance owed. Grandma was retired at that time and on a fixed income, but she went into her retirement savings and paid what was owed.

During my sophomore year, our financial woes took a turn for the worse. Before the year began, I was on the verge of not coming back to the school. I would have had to go to Dunbar High School, where my parents went, which was fine with me. I'd be there with all of my neighborhood friends and I'd sky-rocket up the social ladder. But one day during the end of my freshman year, I went to our mailbox and found a letter addressed to my mother. I read all the mail addressed to her for me, and upon opening the envelope, I discovered a letter that said I had been awarded a full tuition scholarship. You'd think I'd be happy, but I wasn't. I was dejected at the sight of it. I even considered keeping it from Grandma and Bonnie. But how could I do that? There were all the letters Bonnie wrote to the archdiocese on my behalf, and all the sacrifices Grandma had made. Reluctantly, I went in the house and shared the news.

My Gonzaga classmates and I spoke a different language.

After summer vacation one year, I remember being asked by one of my classmates where I summered. Where did I summer? I didn't understand the question. I spent the summer around Hanover. Where else would I be? I later learned that many of my classmates spent the entire summer somewhere other than where they lived during the year. They had summer homes in pretty places and traveled abroad to foreign lands. At my elementary school, I was the only rich kid and the son of a drug dealer at that. But that was many years before, and even then we didn't do the same things that my classmates at Gonzaga did. My parents' perspective was totally different. We came from a place where you got by on your survival instincts. At the time, those same instincts were getting sharper by the day for me, but they didn't quite fit my Gonzaga experience.

I've always been one to handle whatever challenge was placed before me, so I took Gonzaga head on. But my grades from my first few years don't reflect how hard I worked. Many days, I went to school in a heightened emotional state due to something my mother had done the night before or that morning. While at Gonzaga, I once received a report card with notes in the margin that read, "Needs to study more at home." None of my teachers, or my peers for that matter, knew all that I had been through and all that I was going through.

One morning I was in the kitchen buttering some toast in anticipation of going to school when I felt something crash hard into my back. My mother was in the kitchen with me and she had picked up a chair and slammed it into me. "You trying to stab me!" she yelled. Of course I wasn't, but that time I didn't stand around to argue with her. I just left my breakfast on the counter and furiously left the house for school.

Early on, her episodes were bearable, but in the middle of my high school years, her behavior became so erratic and intense that Grandma started seeking help. She learned of an emergency response unit that would come to your home and evaluate your loved one, so she called them and they came out. They found my mother in one of her agitated states and determined that she definitely needed to be taken for more evaluations. So they took her away. Once they evaluated her at the emergency room, they determined that her behavior warranted further tests and treatment, and that's when they committed her to St. Elizabeth.

St. E, as it's called in D.C., is located on Martin Luther King Ave. Going to see my mother there was probably one of the hardest things I've ever had to do. Patients would loiter in front of the building and in the lobbies, so you had to pass through them to enter the facility. Once in the building, you would proceed to the designated floor and then be buzzed onto the ward. Opening the door to the ward, you knew immediately that you had stepped into a different environment, a tilted world.

I've been to see my mother there many times, but that first time was the hardest.

There was a long walkway that led to an open common area. As I started down the walkway immediately to my right, there was a guy answering a pay phone and hanging it up over and over. He kept picking up the receiver, saying, "Hello, who you wanna talk to?" then slamming it back down on the base, but the phone wasn't ringing and he wasn't talking to anybody. Quickly, I figured it must be the phone my mother used when she called Hanover, and when she would call, this strange character was probably over here hovering around her. "One of these crazy motherfuckers best not fuck with my mother," I thought as I continued walking.

There were other patients standing along the walls as I made my way to the nurses' desk in the common area. Some of them carried on conversations with themselves and some were speaking to me as if they knew me, as though we were old friends. One of the nurses and some orderlies were at the nurse station awaiting my arrival. Their desk was next to the common area, so I surveyed the scene. There were patients spread throughout; some were conversing with other patients, some playing cards and chess, and others were in a daze like zombies, just staring off into space. There were patients having loud outbursts and laughing to themselves. While I was taking all that in, the nurse spoke to me and pointed to the place where I could find mom.

There was a series of tables in an adjoining room that had Plexiglas windows. As I entered the room, mom smiled at me with that big pretty smile, showing her gap. She said, "Boobie," which is what she called me sometimes, "they got me fucked up over here ...uh, uh, uh." Her speech was slurred as though her tongue was heavy. The medication she was on had her quite delayed. It reminded me of the dope fiends I'd seen when they were on a good high. She continued talking, "Mama and Bonnie got me over here with all these crazy motherfuckers." I did what I always did. I went right into explaining all the things she had been doing. I told her how she said I wasn't me, slammed the chair into my back, cursed Grandma out, tried to fight Bonnie, and threatened to kill some of the neighbors around the way. But like always, she didn't recall any of her actions. She just went into her routine: "They just jealous because I got money and a Benz and diamond rings...They mad cuz I'm rich."

"Ma, you're not rich," I replied. "We live on Hanover. You got a Mazda 626. The Benz is gone." Then I caught myself because she was nodding in and out.

I had never felt so helpless. I couldn't protect her from what she was going through. After experiencing what I had experienced with my mother over the previous four years, I knew she needed help, but seeing her on a psych ward crushed me. I'd seen my father in prison and that hurt a lot, but it paled in comparison to this—this was my mother. I feared for her because she was in there with what I saw as "real" crazy people, and I couldn't do anything about it. But all in the same moment, I realized that she was like the people there. She had real mental issues that needed to be addressed professionally.

The reality of her situation overwhelmed me, but I refused to break down in front of her. So I prepared to leave so she could go back to her room and rest. I hugged her, told her I loved her, and gave her the clothes and cigarettes she had asked me to bring.

I cried the entire way back across town riding with Grandma, thinking what had happened to the perfect family I had when I was younger. I had gone from having two loving parents in my household to one doing a life sentence in federal prison on the other side of the country and one being committed to a mental institution.

But Mom wouldn't stay there. She returned home about a month after that first visit.

By 1995, when I was fifteen years old, the greater majority of the crew was heavy in the life. There's a saying where I'm from that goes, "Ain't no boys out in the street." Everyone in the life and, for that matter, everyone hanging out around it is a man. If you were thirteen, you'd better be prepared to act thirty because in all situations that's how old you'll be treated.

We started to take on members from the crew from the northeast side of North Capitol Street around the time that most of our crew was getting into the life. In D.C., there are North Capitol, South Capitol, and East Capitol streets. These streets separate D.C. into its four quadrants of northwest, northeast, southeast, and southwest. With North Capitol Street being so close, the northeast guys we took into our crew were from our neighborhood. They literally lived across the street on the northeast side of North Capitol. But in D.C. we looked for any excuse to separate ourselves from others, so much so that
104

guys that lived across the street, but technically lived in another quadrant, were viewed as being from somewhere else. Initially, we saw the northeast guys in the crew as much more timid than us. They included Kenny, Mike Bradshaw, Alan and Kevin Powell, Chaz, Dave Suede, Son-Son, and James Whitaker. They would hang on North Capitol between O and P. We merged into the 1st and O—NCO (North Capitol and O) crew.

Within both crews, the great majority of the guys dealt cocaine. Cocaine and crack cocaine are one and the same. The difference is that crack is made by adding an alkali (for example, baking soda) to the cocaine and cooking it in water. This process hardens the drug into rock form and allows it to be smoked. That's it. It's that simple. The demonization of crack came not because it was all that different from powder cocaine, but because the violence surrounding crack became different.

In the U.S., cocaine started out as a rather exclusive drug because it was expensive. But as the market became super saturated and crack became popular, the cost of the drug plummeted. Now with an overabundance of the drug, anyone could afford to buy it and anyone, like my friends in 1st and O, could afford to sell it.

At the height of the cocaine epidemic, rock cocaine was smoked by all classes of people. The popular name "crack" arose when the method of use became associated with the poor, more specifically with poor urban blacks. When that happened, cocaine users of means disavowed crack. Publicly, smoking crack became taboo. Privately, however, affluent users still turned to the pipe. The high was too good, and having money helps to all the better hide vice and affliction.

Freebasing crack cocaine produces a brief but euphoric high. In neighborhoods like mine all over the country, you had great numbers of downhearted people open to try anything that would bring them up. They tried crack, it made them feel great, and it wasn't long before they were hooked. Nothing is instantly addictive, but the intense feeling of happiness and confidence that crack produced caught on quickly with the dispossessed. Users in communities like the one I grew up in created an intense demand for crack, and it led to the worst kind of idolatry. People worshipped the high and the money made in supplying the high.

Because crack highs are short but intense, users had to go back again and again for the drug. This overwhelming demand drastically altered the economy and the ethics of the ghetto. It produced a tipping point. Getting high and getting money truly became a fanatic cult where devotees would defend their right to worship at all costs. More money for the dealers meant more access to guns—big guns with long clips in the hands of all the fanatics. A rival dealer trying to take over another dealer's territory was like desecrating that dealer's god, an offense corrected only by murder. From the dealer's standpoint, anything getting in the way of him getting money, whether it was one dollar or one million dollars, was an offense punishable by death. This philosophy infected the communities that dealers operated in as much as the drugs they were dealing. Fistfights became gunfights. Worse yet, insult and casual slight became reason enough to take a human life. Killing had become cultural. This is what made the crack era so remarkable. There have been other drug epidemics in this country, but none that made killing so normal.

The saturation of cocaine in the U.S. and the introduction of crack quickly broke down the need for large-scale and organized drug operations. The organizations headed by so-called kingpins still existed, but with so much cocaine available, there were many more independent mid-level and low-level dealers. Old codes were no longer respected by these younger men who came up differently than their elder criminal counterparts. Hierarchal strongholds broke down and chaos ensued. This is one of the reasons D.C. became so violent.

My father and Rayful going to prison in 1989 created a vacuum that hundreds of these mid- and low-level dealers rushed to fill. In addition to those from D.C., you had New York City hustlers and even crews from Jamaica competing for corners. So in some neighborhoods you had drug wars with Washingtonians pitted against each other and in other neighborhoods they warred with outsiders. Washingtonian dealers battling with outsiders for territory began to say "D.C." stood for "Don't Come." You had this kind of thing happening all across the country.

Yet, territory and the economics of crack don't fully explain the steady murder rate of D.C. in the 1990s, nor do they explain the killing today in cities like Chicago. Murder rates are falling precipitously in big cities across the country, most notably New York City, but Chicago and other cities that have this problem are still struggling.

I watched killing become cultural in my neighborhood. I watched as my friends went from frightened and sometimes timid little boys to stone-cold killers turned off to innocence and turned out by the gun. Any altercation could become deadly. Too often, before my eyes, things did.

I was ten years old the first time someone my age that I knew from our neighborhood got shot and killed. His name was Charles, and he lived on N Street, a block away from Hanover. Charles was only a few years older than me, but he liked to hang with the older crowd. He was good friends with one of the big homies of the block named Moe Man. One day Moe Man and Charles were admiring Moe Man's new .45 caliber pistol, handling it and aiming it, when the gun discharged, striking Charles in the head and killing him. In shock, Moe Man fled the scene. When word spread that Charles was dead, everyone on Hanover and in its immediate area was devastated.

Charles's death was an accident, but Moe Man ended up doing time for his friend's death. As a ten year old, I didn't know then that seeing death would become a way of life for me. Nothing could prepare me for the ultimate—the times I have had to see fallen friends, dying right there before me. I'm talking about close friends, friends who I was just with, lying before me on the pavement, never to rise again. Lil' Dennis was the first.

Within the 1st and O crew, I became closest with my friends Shakey, Jerome, and Fat Man. But before Lil' Dennis jumped off the porch and got heavy into the life, he and I were very close. Not that we weren't close when he was hustling; I saw him almost every day. It's just I didn't hustle, so the majority of our time was spent differently. Lil' Dennis was a year older than me. He was wiry with ears that poked out a little. He had fair skin and a smile that would light up his entire face. He also had a slight deformity on his left hand and bad asthma.

One weekend my mother took me and Lil' Dennis to Atlantic City to enjoy the boardwalk and the Jersey Shore. This was in the early 1990s before my mother's condition prevented her from doing things like that for me. Thinking back, I don't know where my mother got the money to take us. Though Atlantic City is only a few hours from D.C., a simple trip like the one we took solely on a bus driver's salary was the highest of luxury, a far cry from the days my father was home. But, as I said before, my mother held on to those days, trying in vain to keep them alive.

Anyway, the sun was shining and the boardwalk was full of people. Lil' Dennis and I walked it, taking in the sights, while Mom gambled in the casino. As we were walking, Lil' Dennis had a bad asthma attack. He fell down, gasping for air. He had left his inhaler in the hotel room. I'd never seen his asthma hit him so badly and, in my young mind, I thought he was going to die. Dennis had all but collapsed onto the boardwalk and a little crowd formed around us. One of those guys with a rickshaw-like

109

buggy offered his help. He and I loaded Lil' Dennis in it and pushed him back to the hotel as if it were an ambulance. I kept looking at Dennis to see if he was okay. He was wheezing something serious. I prayed he'd be all right. Dramatically, we made it into our hotel room and to his inhaler. After a number of puffs of the inhaler and deep inhalations, Lil' Dennis recovered. He came back quickly, and we laughed and joked about the incident together.

In about a year's time after our trip to Atlantic City, Lil' Dennis had changed, all his boyishness removed. That's how quickly the metamorphosis happens in the hood. Though his asthma wasn't as bad anymore, Dennis didn't stop carrying his inhaler. Now he carried it in his pocket next to the gun he strapped against his hip.

Lil' Dennis and Stinka started to get tight around the time Dennis jumped off the porch. Stinka was one of the youngest of the crew, but he always carried himself like a man. He and Lil' Dennis went to Shaw Junior High School together. At Shaw, junior high goes from the seventh grade to the ninth grade. Lil' Dennis was in ninth grade, and Stinka was in seventh when, one day, some dudes from 7th Street (the 1512 building, which was near Shaw) jumped them. Surviving a brawl will strengthen the bonds between you and your friends. The altercation with the guys from 7th Street crew did just that for Dennis and Stinka, but it also did something else. It prompted Stinka to get his first gun, a .22 caliber pistol, and proceed to shoot at the guys that jumped them.

Stinka's transformation started then, as a thirteen year old in the seventh grade. After shooting at someone for the first time, he didn't immediately start carrying a gun every day, but the love affair started in that moment, and eventually he'd start carrying weapons and using firearms as though that were his purpose in life.

I've seen it happen too many times—young men from neighborhoods like the one I'm from being turned out by the gun. In the hood, possessing the power of a firearm makes you feel different. It's a different kind of high. The gun makes young men from the hood go from feeling powerless to their circumstances to powerful—invisible to invincible. It gives the guy in the neighborhood who lacks confidence something to feel supremely confident about. The gun, as strange as it may sound, provides clarity. If I point this at you and pull it, bang, you'll die, or if not you'll certainly know that I am here. Sadly, for the young killer or would-be killer, death and the prospect of death becomes the greatest affirmation of life. As killing becomes cultural, this avowal blends into speech, the various colloquialisms of the street: "Them dudes over there be puttin' in work" (they're here). "Better know, we let them things spray" (we're here). "Nigga, I'll bust your ass" (I'm here).

People complain about the violence in hip-hop music, but the music only reflects this real culture. Rappers take kernels of things they hear and see on the street or heard and saw from someone from the street and make a creative rhyme about it over a beat. That's it. Critics of these lyrics continually fail or refuse to look deeper. Better to be upset about the culture of violence and why it persists rather than spending any time talking about music and entertainment. The greatest solutions, by far, are found and will continue to be found in proactive work in changing the culture of violence in neighborhoods that breed young killers. I know because the purveyors of the culture were my friends. I saw and touched their weapons: Desert Eagles, Mac-10s, AK-47s. Military arms used to hunt the enemy. I used to look in their eyes and see the deadly reverence they had for it. I'd hear it in their talk, the way they'd excitedly imitate the sound and the rhythm of the guns blasting "boom-boomboomboomboomboomboomboomboom" as if describing an exciting play on the football field, but these were the killing fields, and I was on them.

We saw death and decay both inside and outside of our homes. We saw traditions and values that once fortified the poor and oppressed rotting away for faster pleasures. We weren't valued because we were the future—the only thing of value in our time was the present. How can I be gratified right now? The little things, those small but gratifying things children do day to day, weren't enough. They weren't overtly powerful enough. Appreciating those things takes patience, and the generation that was rearing us wasn't patient enough. Synthetic things were finally opening up to us, and coupled with the oppressions and distractions of old, we, the new generation, their children, were left to raise ourselves. This isn't an excuse for the violence, but it's the truth. When you have a teenager committing murder, questions must be asked of his environment and how he was reared in it. My generation suffered from regression. On our blocks, very little grew, was strengthened, or furthered from the previous generation aside from anger. A good example of this in my neighborhood was our war with Sursum Corda.

The irony found in the naming of big city housing projects of the 1960s has occurred to me. Very often, the places begin with a glimmer of hope. The buildings are shiny and new with apartments filled with amenities that seem fantastic when compared to the residents' previous slum-living conditions. They stand proudly at first but are propped-up on specious promise and eventually fall to disrepair and destitution. Hanover neighbors two such places: Tyler House where my good friend Scoop used to live, a place where recently thirteen people were shot in a drive-by, and Sursum Corda Cooperative.

Sursum Corda is Latin for *lift up your hearts* or *hearts lifted.* The phrase is rooted in the Eucharistic prayer of the Christian church. The Sursum Corda Cooperative, which we call "the Cordas," is a 199-unit housing project built in 1968. In my parents' generation, the Cordas was looked at as an extension of Hanover. We were from the same neighborhood and bound together. That would change with my generation as our lives contracted. Old allies became natural enemies.

My man Alan Powell, who was a member of 1st and O, got into a disagreement with a much older guy from Sursum Corda over a dice game. The guy from Sursum Corda roughed

Alan off, which is D.C. slang for someone being taken advantage of by force. Alan was much younger than this guy from Sursum Corda, and he wasn't one to really bring the drama, but Stinka would. By that point, Stinka had earned a reputation for busting his gun. With Lil' Dennis and Stinka being close, Dennis was right there with Stinka ready to stand up for Alan, our crew, and our hood. Remember, respect meant everything, and displays of weakness had to be reconciled immediately. This happened in 1996, which was one of Washington, D.C.'s most murderous years.

Lil' Dennis was a full-time hustler then. Almost overnight he went from borrowing my clothes to wear to school (we went to separate high schools, and at Gonzaga I wore a uniform) to having his own fresh gear to wear, to getting things I was not able to get. I'm thinking specifically of his Air Jordan 11 playoff editions. The original black and white shoe was extremely popular. The clean and glowing appearance of the sneaker, accented by black patent leather at its toe, compelled guys to wear them with their suits and tuxedos to prom and had other prom goers buzzing about the fashion statement. But the black and red playoff editions took the furor over the shoe to another level. This was Michael Jordan's full comeback year, the record-breaking seventy-two-win season, and the shoes were hot but they were also expensive. To get them before they sold out, you had to have the money right now, and I did not. I couldn't afford them, and that was hard for me to swallow.

I didn't work a job all through high school. It wasn't that I was lazy. My not working had everything to do with my perspective and my family dynamics. I spent my first nine years getting anything and everything I wanted, but when my father went to prison, all of that ended. I was still accustomed to getting everything I wanted, like my mother, but to a lesser extent. I'm not going to complain about how tough we had it financially when my father went away. I know there are those who viewed my father as a drug dealer, and therefore felt our fall was expected and perhaps just. Still, I had to make some psychological adjustments. However the money came, I was born into it. I'd be disingenuous if I didn't admit that for a while I missed our old lifestyle. My father came attached with it all, and it's fair to say I associated my time with him in freedom, and my mother on the lucid side of her illness, with all the luxury. The travel, the fine dining, the fancy clothes, it all came with them. But how badly could I miss going to eat at expensive restaurants when I watched my friends from the neighborhood frequent S.O.M.E. (So Others Might Eat), the local food depository? Their fathers were gone, too, and their mothers were afflicted. I've always been perceptive, and I was taught to count my blessings, so it didn't take me a long time to realize despite my losses that I was relatively privileged.

My mother always cooked what I wanted to eat when we didn't go out, but Grandma was different. She didn't always ask me what I wanted to eat. Most days I didn't care because she'd cook something I liked. But when she would cook liver, lima beans, and pigs' feet, I'd object. One of our exchanges in these moments I remember clearly. Grandma had prepared a less-than-desirable meal, and I looked at her and said, "Grandma, I don't eat that." The nerve! Grandma was quick with a come-back. She said, "When your ass goes to jail, you will eat whatev-er they feed you!" Lord knows she didn't want that to be my fate, but I think that deep down she expected it. Her uncon-scious mind was speaking. Going to prison had been the fate of so many of the young men around her, including her own children, Boo and Gregory. Then you had my father and Cornell and probably a hundred more neighborhood boys she knew, like Tall Reds and the Wilson brothers.

But Grandma understood just how much I was dealing with. So when she made chitterlings or pigs' feet or liver or any other food I found undesirable, she started fixing me something separate or would go buy me something.

I think my getting money from Grandma from time to time as well as from my aunt and uncles also prevented me from getting a job. Why would I get a job when they'd give me money, and I could take that money and go shoot dice to make more money? I also didn't see getting up and going to work from the men in my family or, for that matter, the men in the neighborhood. Despite what had happened to my father and all of his admonishments and warnings from prison such as, "Son, watch what you do and watch who you be with," at the time I thought working a job was for suckers. Sometimes when my father would issue those warnings to me I'd think, "Dog, do you know where I live? It's the same block you grew up on!" But not

116

only on the block was crime happening, it was happening in my home.

Uncle Greg was released from prison around my sophomore year of high school. He had been incarcerated my entire life, and once his sentence was up, having him back home was a delight. Outside the visiting room, there were no restrictions, and I was able to experience whole other sides of him. Bonding with him was good for me because it gave me another strong male family member to compare myself to, to question, and to look up to. He lived with us for a short while, so I could easily observe his mannerisms, and I absorbed them all. Greg liked to use the word "Joe" when referring to someone. "Joe" was a part of D.C. slang (I've heard it's Chicago slang, too), but Uncle Greg made it sound like his own.

Uncle Greg, institutionalized for so long, brought his prison habits home, such as eating ravenously. I'd look up from my plate, and he'd be finished. He also had a habit of reporting everything that he was about to do. We'd be together and he'd say, "Joe, I'll be right back. I'm about to go upstairs real quick to get this laundry." Or "Joe, I'll be right back. I'm about to go take a piss." The bathroom thing cracked me up. One day I had to tell him that it was all right and that he didn't have to tell me each time that he was going to relieve himself.

Uncle Greg worked a job for a while, but the meager wages and the conditions he saw around him drove him back to his old habit. I remember the first time he clued me in that he was back at it. It was right around Thanksgiving, and he and I were having

117

a moment together at Grandma's when he turned to me, nodded his head, and said, "Joe, we gon be all right for Christmas." Sure enough, a month or so later he came over to the house and gave me a stack of envelopes full of money, telling me to pass them out to everyone on Christmas Day. Greg had written each family member's name on his or her individual envelope. We had a big family, but Greg didn't just pass out money to us. He gave money to many people throughout the neighborhood. He'd hear about a family that was having a hard time, and he'd give them money. We celebrate Robin Hood in stories, but the real-life version isn't so romantic. But that's what Greg was. I'm not excusing my uncle's behavior. The money came from robbing banks. Bank robbery is a serious crime, which can be deadly. But this is my family's truth.

Uncle Greg never killed anyone during any of his bank robberies, but he did get shot once. I saw the fresh wound. It happened in an armored truck heist. He had recruited some guys that weren't built for the job, and things got messy. The truck driver fired shots at Greg, and a bullet caught him underneath his vest. After his crew escaped the scene, he went to be patched up by a friend's wife, who happened to be a nurse, then came around Hanover. Inside Grandma's house, Uncle Greg pulled up his shirt, showing me the wound as he shared with me what had happened.

Another time, Uncle Greg came home after a robbery with a big duffle bag full of money. He entrusted me with it, telling me to put it up and he'd be back for it. The moment made me feel proud. It's strange to say now, but it's completely true for that time in my life. It meant he trusted me. It meant he respected me. He knew I wouldn't tell, and I wasn't one to run my mouth. He knew all the things I had seen with my father, but he had also been watching me when he came home. What code did I live by? I wasn't a criminal, but I knew the code. I also knew what inevitably came with that code. After being home for seven years, in 2001, Uncle Greg was caught, tried, and convicted to a life sentence in prison.

Now, even when Uncle Greg was home, there often wasn't a surplus of money. He wasn't robbing banks once a week, and when he did he often gave most of it away. Also, I rarely asked my family for money, especially as I got older. But if they gave it to me, fine. Again, my family wasn't as needy as other families. But there's the basic level of need that exists in the hood, and then there's the psychological want that feels like need. In the hood, dressing nicely and having the latest things often feels like a need. Having the latest this or that makes you feel better about yourself and projects the illusion of wellness and prosperity to others. The show is highly respected, and the girls check for it, which creates a powerful psychological pull where I come from. So something like a pair of sneakers can send a young man over the edge.

I had a lot of material things as a child, but I was raised to keep those things in the proper perspective. This was reinforced when it was all taken away. So, as a teenager, I wasn't as affected by the pull as others, but I still was affected. When my

119

homies started hustling and suddenly I was no longer the sharpest dressed and I didn't have a car and I couldn't get the latest things, it bothered me. At times, I'd be close to stepping off that edge, but someone in my family or a friend of the family would always come through with a little money to hold me back. For years, since I was around twelve years old, my father's friends would bring money to me to give to him. The amounts varied, but let's say they gave me five hundred dollars. When my father called from prison, I'd report how much I was given, and he'd say, "Okay, send me half and you keep half." I'd then take the cash to the post office to send to him. A USPS money order was required to send federal prisoners money. Then, with me still being accustomed to having things and with that need to have things ever present, my portion of the money would be gone in no time. Every time, I burned right through it. When I was a small child, I'd regularly be given hundred-dollar bills as if they were dollar bills. That past, coupled with the pressures of my environment as a teenager, made two hundred and fifty dollars feel like loose change in my pocket.

But these occasions were spotted and very spread out through my adolescence. So when the black and red Jordan 11s came out and I didn't have the money to get them, it bothered me, but by then not having things wasn't strange to me. Still, the shoes sure looked good on Lil' Dennis's feet.

By the summer of 1996, at sixteen years of age, Lil' Dennis had a child and one on the way, a car, fresh clothes, and a firm commitment to meet aggression with aggression. In the streets, he was a man. In retaliation for Alan Powell, he and Stinka shot at the guy from Sursum Corda who violated. They didn't hit him. Either way, hit or not hit, Stinka and Dennis knew it was on. Someone from Sursum Corda would be coming around our way to strike back at them. They just didn't know when.

Sometimes, when the beef is on, you'll get a word about what your rivals were up to and an approximation of when they planned on making a move. The night Dennis died, we received no such word. It was around eleven o'clock, and like always I was outside with the crew. I remember Dennis and me talking as we always would, and him showing me his gun. After a while, for some reason, I left the corner and went home for a few minutes. I didn't have a curfew or anything and it wasn't that late. I don't know why I went home. Not long after I had stepped foot inside, the word got to me that Lil' Dennis had been shot. I flew out the house, racing to the scene. What I found is really hard to put into words. Dennis's lifeless body was lying beside the stoop on O Street where he and I were just talking. How can I describe the feeling? The best word is "powerless." Seeing him lying there, bleeding out on the pavement, it felt like all the energy in my body had been sucked out of me. Everything felt weak—all my limbs, my heart. When you see someone you were close to die in that way, a part of you leaves, never to return. What's worse is that Dennis's death was the beginning of a deadly feud that would last three years, a feud that resulted in many deaths. Now sides don't matter, only the lost souls. Tia was the next to die. She was from Sursum Corda and supposedly was the lookout that got Dennis killed. Stinka was charged with her murder and is now serving time for it. Young women are often just as wrapped-up in the madness, either as participants or innocent bystanders.

Out of the 1st and O crew, I was closest to Shakey, Fat Man, and Jerome in high school. For a time Shakey and I were inseparable. Shakey was tall and skinny with big hands, big feet, and curly hair, and he was dark, about my complexion. There was something about Shake that made us extremely tight, but I can't quite identify it. Perhaps one of the reasons was because he and I internalized our hurt similarly. While I was more of a fighter and unleashed my fury with my fists too many times to count, Shakey wasn't a punk. He was mostly good natured, laid back, and funny, but if you rubbed him the wrong way, he'd go off on anybody. He didn't care if they had a reputation for being a killer, Shakey would snap when he felt severely wronged. It didn't happen a lot, but what he had been through might have been an excuse for it.

At around the age of seven, Shakey saw his mother shot to death by her boyfriend. He then went to live with his father and his aunt at his aunt's house. His aunt had a son named Tim. Though different, Tim and Shakey were very close and were more like brothers. Tim and his mom were there for Shakey when his father died young, right in their home, from complications having to do with diabetes and drug addiction.

Tim would eventually turn to the street, but Shakey didn't. Like me, Shakey was out there, but he didn't participate in the criminal life. We did things that were by the books illegal, of course, but there's a difference between teenage mischief and living an illegal life. In an understood way, I think this is why Shakey, Jerome, Fat Man, and I grew closer.

For the four of us, going to school every day helped to keep us out of some trouble. While most of the crew had dropped out and were in the street nearly all day, we went to school faithfully. Shakey had perfect attendance in junior high and high school despite being held back three times in one grade and never finishing high school. He had gotten too old and the school board eventually forced him to leave. His record still reflects that he had perfect attendance though. We joke about that sometimes. We also joke about the times we were together when my mom was having an episode. I had to learn to laugh to cope. Shakey and the guys helped me with that. They'd laugh at me, and eventually with me, about my mother. They had a right to. Fat Man endured all kinds of humiliation because of his mother's addiction, and Shakey's mother was no longer with us. We were brothers, kindred spirits who were surviving it all together.

Once, around Christmas time, Shakey and I were in our house when Mom started acting up. She had come to confront me in the living room where Shakey and I were relaxing. Grandma had put up our Christmas tree and had decorated the room nicely, like always. Normally, I would be cool when my mother flared up, but this time I couldn't hold my frustration in. There was a football at my feet. Yelling back at my mother, I picked up the football and fired it into the Christmas tree. The ball went through the tree and crashed through the front window. I didn't intend for that to happen.

Grandma's reaction was swift. She rushed in the living room and proceeded to put my mother, Shakey, the dog, and me all out of the house. It was cold outside and miserable, and of course, my mother continued ranting, but because Shakey was there it was funny. Grandma even kicked the dog out. It might not have been funny in the moment, but the incident became one of those times that we always look back at and laugh about.

Another time, Fat Man was there along with Shakey. My mother drove the five of us to the pharmacy to put in her prescription. She sent us into the store while she waited in the car. After getting the medicine, we all returned to the car. Before turning the car on, my mother asked me what address I had given the pharmacist. Now, there was only one address that I could give them, 39 Hanover Place. So I said, "Ma, I gave them our address." When I said that she began to hit me repeatedly, saying, "You dumb stupid motherfucker! Now they going to come kill us!" When she had beaten me sufficiently and started to drive, the barrage of "dumb stupid motherfuckers...they gon kill us" continued. All I could do was take it. Again, not funny in the moment, but because of Fat Man and Shakey, the memory would become hilarious. Fat Man and Shakey would often make fun of me by impersonating Mom, and that time in the car gave them more material. They would reenact the scene as if it were a skit, one person playing me and the other playing Mom, and

124

seeing them act it out would crack me up every time.

Fat Man was an accomplished band member at Dunbar High School. With his talents in the band and the support of the Gold Coast people that went to his church, he became the first guy from our hood to go to college. He went to Johnson C. Smith University in Charlotte, North Carolina. For two years, he did well there, but in 1999 during the spring break of his junior year, his life and our relationship would change forever.

It happened on March 5th. I was in my room with my girl-friend, Tracie, watching TV when the phone rang. I picked up the receiver and listened to the voice on the other end tell me the terrible news. Tim and Fat Man had been horse playing when things turned serious. An argument ensued that prompted Fat Man to angrily storm off to his house. Unexpectedly, Fat Man reemerged with a kitchen knife and stabbed Tim in the chest.

I quickly told Tracie what had happened, told her to stay put, and, again, ran to the scene. Fat Man had fled, and Tim was lying on the ground unconscious and bleeding heavily. The paramedics came and, in shock, we all watched as they tried in vain to save him. Fat Man had plunged the knife into Tim's aorta, and the medics could not stop the bleeding. We watched Tim die.

How could Fat Man do it? Sure, there was division among the crew, but for the most part we were all close. We were 1st and O. That meant something. Didn't it? I was furious with Fat Man. Shakey wanted him dead. It was sad because I was torn between my two best friends. I had major love for Fat Man and I understood what brought on the tragic moment. He was a gentle soul who never was known for violence, but the pressure of our environment, all that we saw and survived, his mother's addiction and her embarrassing actions, the ridicule and the shame that came with it all, was too much for him to take, and in that moment arguing with Tim, he reached his breaking point.

In the aftermath, I was estranged from Fat Man. I was terribly upset and disappointed in him, and I felt I could no longer trust him. If he'd kill Tim, then he'd kill me, at least that was the rationale I forced myself to believe. Shakey also needed me more than him. He had lost his own blood, a first cousin who was like a brother.

I couldn't have predicted that less than ten years later I'd know the exact feeling.

Fat Man beat his court case. He lived in the hood but never took to the streets. Tim did and had a criminal record. Fat Man's lawyers painted a picture of two very different young men: the vicious thug versus the gentle schoolboy, but Fat Man and Tim were from the same place, and there are no angels where I'm from. How could there be when we were living in hell? Still, it's easier for people to think of all of us in that way, to paint the troubled ones with a broad stroke. Then we are easier to dismiss from conscience. Ironically, right before Tim died, he had just gotten a job. He was hustling, and hustlers don't get jobs, but he did. Perhaps it signaled a change of heart. Maybe he was trying to let the streets go. Yet, we will never know how honest work would have impacted him. It may have done nothing, but it also could have done a lot. I've seen it.

I've often thought that if I was there that day, Tim would still be alive and Fat Man and I would still be friends. I used to feel the same way about my man Scoop who took his own life a year before Tim died. Scoop had moved away from Tyler House to Maryland, but we kept in close communication. He'd come back around Hanover from time to time and was shown love because everyone knew him as my good boyhood friend. During high school, we also talked on the phone weekly. He came around looking for me the day he committed suicide. Ironically, Tim was the one to tell me there was some news about Scoop getting shot and to go home to find out the whole story. I wish I was there when Scoop came looking for me. Maybe he was just coming to say goodbye without saying it, or maybe I could have lifted him up. Maybe the things we would have talked about would have reminded Scoop that he had something to live for. These kinds of thoughts on my friends' pointless deaths haunted me for a long time.

Rites of Passage

The 1990s were rough. Once a day, I'd get on my knees and pray these simple words, "God, please help me to help myself." Immediately after that, I'd pray the Hail Mary: *Hail Mary, full of Grace, the Lord is with thee. Blessed are thou among women and blessed is the fruit of thy womb, Jesus. Holy Mary, Mother of God, pray for us sinners now and at the hour of our death. Amen.*

This is all I knew to do. I'm thankful that my family was also there with me to help me through.

I used to look at Rayful like a family member. I would go visit him in prison sometimes with his girlfriend Vicki and his son, Little Rayful. He was incarcerated about four hours from D.C. in Lewisburg, the same prison Uncle Greg was in. They were together there for a while. I remember going to Lewisburg and wishing my father had been that close because at the time he was incarcerated in California.

Rayful would call me often from prison. He'd ask how my dad was doing and how I was doing. He had a friend that managed an Athlete's Foot, and he would send me there to get tennis shoes from the guy. Sometimes we'd call famous athletes that he knew. But that wasn't all he'd do. He also had me call people for him, sometimes long distance numbers, and ask me to put the phone down for five or ten minutes.

From 1990 to 1996, I took regular calls from Rayful. But then one day he called and said that we would hear something about him in the media. "Just know I had my reasons," he said, ending our conversation. Shortly after that talk, the local news announced that he had cooperated with the government. He had set up other drug dealers on the street for unconfirmed concessions and was now in the Witness Protection Program. Uncle Ray had become the enemy: a snitch, a rat, a non-entity. Just like that, he had to be dead to me. Yet I still had so many unresolved feelings. This was a man I had come to care for. In a way, our interactions after he and my father went to prison helped to buoy me. My dad was on the other side of the country, but Rayful was close, and the familiarity of our interactions substituted for something like paternal care.

After my father went to prison, I lost nearly all contact with his side of the family and many of my father's friends. In an instant, I went from seeing Rico and Antonio all the time to seeing them very infrequently; the same went for Lou, Aunt Barbara, and the rest. My dad was the glue, and he was the only person Rico and Antonio would listen to. Their mischievousness was relatively innocent compared to the things they got involved in once my dad left. He gave them much more structure than their parents were able to provide and, in a way, my father acted as their paternal figure as well. Given the tumult of their everyday world, he had been the one reliable and steady presence. They were tough boys, but I know they wouldn't be in prison had my dad not been locked away. But he was, and they were, too—that's how the cycle works.

As I watched the news report about Rayful becoming an informant, I felt yet another loss. I also, almost immediately, thought about all those phone calls he used to have me make. I wondered if I inadvertently helped set up deals with those calls to strange numbers, those times he asked me to put the phone down. I had flashbacks of the times I'd eavesdropped and heard conversations I didn't understand. I was a boy then. At twelve, thirteen, fourteen, even at sixteen, I was wise to some of the ways of the world, specifically the world I knew, but I was not a man. I never told my father about those calls I made for Rayful. I knew just the thought of Rayful even potentially involving me would enrage him.

Rayful's cooperation was big news in the hood. Around my way, I don't know how many times I heard variations of the following two statements: "I don't know why Tony fuck with that nigga anyway; he not a Hanover nigga." And "Tony ain't need that nigga."

I went to see my father in California for the second time not long after Rayful flipped. It was Thanksgiving, 1996, and it had been four years since I had last seen him. I was sixteen years old and had matured a lot. My father was no longer with Karen, so I was accompanied this time by a different one of his girlfriends, a woman I didn't know at the time. I was far less emotional on that trip, so I was able to take a lot more in. Lompoc was in the middle of nowhere, like most maximum-security prisons. To get

131

there, we flew into LAX then took a small plane to Santa Barbara. From Santa Barbara, there was an hour cab ride to Lompoc. On the way to the prison, we passed Michael Jackson's Neverland Ranch. When the cab driver pointed it out, I got excited. I hadn't realized it was in the area because when I was twelve we had taken a different route, flying into Santa Maria instead.

Unlike my trip with Karen and Rico, this time I was able to have some time alone with my dad. His girlfriend understood the importance of that. I was far more vigilant on that visit than the first. I was much more aware of the guards and their treatment of the inmates, seeing how they monitor the visits. They were not friendly. During that visit, I became fully aware of prison culture. My father pointed out inmates involved in homosexual relationships though their wife and kids were visiting. I saw a woman caught smuggling drugs to her boyfriend who owed debts. I also learned about prison gangs. We've never had a gang culture in D.C.; it's always been about crews and blocks, and beyond that there's an individualist culture in the D.C. streets. But California had a very prominent gang culture, and in the visiting room my father showed me who was what and what that meant. He talked to me about Bloods and Crips, the Mexican Mafia, and the Aryan Brotherhood, who had a longstanding hatred for D.C. blacks stemming from an incident that happened at USP Lewisburg in the early 1970s.

Of course, we talked about Rayful becoming an informant. Though he and Rayful's relationship strained after they went to prison, out of respect, Rayful had called him too right before the news came out, saying virtually the same thing he said to me. My father thought someone had died because you don't get calls in prison.

On that visit, I also met Carmine Persico, boss of the Colombo crime family. His family was staying at the same hotel as us, and one morning I bumped into them and we exchanged pleasantries. I didn't know who they were at the time, just that they were from New York and were dressed nice. The family happened to be in the visiting room while I was there waiting for my father to come out. I went to the vending machine to get some things for him before he came out, and I walked past their table. One of Carmine's family members pointed out that we were in the same hotel and that we had had a polite chat, so Carmine nodded at me and said, "How you doing, young man?" When my dad came out, he and Carmine greeted one another warmly, and then he explained to me that Carmine was in the mob and that he was the gardener at the prison. He didn't say anything about Carmine being the boss. My dad doesn't talk that way. I later made the connection for myself when watching a mob program on the cable station A&E.

In addition to catching up with me and enjoying one another, my father was intent on demonstrating to me the truth of prison life. He wanted to educate me and made it abundantly clear why I never wanted to be where he was. As he constantly reminded me when we spoke by telephone, he reaffirmed the importance of watching whom I spent my time with and watching what I did. But, again, it was easy for him to say that, to envision me as the child that I was when he left me. I'd tell him about my friends dying, but he didn't know them and things had changed dramatically since he went away, so it was hard for him to envision it. He had no frame of reference for either what was happening to my mother or what was happening to my generation on the streets. And while doing his time, psychologically, it was easier to imagine me safe. I was not safe, but I understood what my father was going through, and as I got older, in many ways, I tried to protect him too. I didn't want to burden him with my problems.

I tried my best to heed my father's advice and to make Grandma and Aunt Bonnie proud. But I wasn't going to stay inside. All of my friends were out in the streets, and I was going to be out there with them. That was who I was and who I always had been. The habits that I had picked up from being around my father and my uncles were deeply ingrained in me. For example, I loved shooting dice, but the crap game was an incredibly dangerous place to be. You had to deal with ass betters, stick-up boys, police, sore losers, etc. Also, the money kept your attention, so you could never be fully focused at crap games, and your enemies could capitalize on that—and they did.

Once, a bunch of us from 1st and O—Shakey was definitely there—were playing craps on the side of an abandoned school in our neighborhood. This was in the summer of 1998, and I had just graduated from Gonzaga High School. The school was one of our spots to gamble. It had a nice playing surface and was kind of tucked away and fenced in, which gave it a more secluded feel. Along with guys from 1st and O, girls from the neighborhood were also out there watching the game. The school was an old brick building. We were gambling next to the side entrance. I was standing with my back to the door and under an archway when I happened to glance to my right toward the street. The street was about thirty yards away. I saw a car and something sticking out of it that caught the light and shined. I recognized it as a gun and only had time to say "O!" and step back into the entrance for cover before shots started ringing out at us. We were pinned. Bullets slammed into the brick right next to my face, and the shots would not stop coming. People in front of me, who didn't have my cover, were falling to the ground and stumbling over one another trying to find safety. The bullets kept coming—just showering. I don't know how many guns or what kind of guns they had on us, but I'd never heard that many shots and haven't since. The shots seemed to go on forever.

When they finally stopped, we all ran out of there. Incredibly, no one was seriously injured; a couple of people got shot and a girl's face got trampled in the scramble to get out of there, but when everyone was accounted for, the injury toll was minor compared to what it could have been. It was a crew from the Cordas, and it's frightening to think had they come down the alley in the car, which instead of thirty yards to the side was directly in front of us, we might have all been dead.

Another time, me, Shakey, our guy Brock, and two other big homies, Trump and Russell, were shooting the dice, when, out of nowhere, a guy from the Cordas walked up to Brock, put a gun to his head, and pulled the trigger. The gun didn't fire. It clicked. It had jammed. Before I knew it, Shakey had sprung up and ran. Trump ran too. Russell got face down on the ground (he thought it was a robbery), and Brock was fighting with the guy with the gun. I froze in indecision. Should I run or help Brock fight? In that instance, my flight instincts won out. I started running in Shakey's direction down the alley. He had a good lead on me. Shakey was tall and slim and floated over the ground as he ran. I watched him leap over something and then heard the sound of gunfire behind me. I was already running fast, but upon hearing the sound, my body shifted into another gear I didn't know I had. Were the shots coming for me? Was this it? Not knowing if you're going to live or die is a terrible feeling. I was running for my life.

I lost Shakey; at some point, he had turned one way and I turned the other. I came out of the alley and into a clearing and ducked into Steve's, a corner store on 1st and P. Waiting there for a moment and looking out the door, I saw Brock hobbling in my direction. He was shot, but he was clear from the shooter. I left the store and went to give him some support. He had been shot in the leg, and it was bleeding heavily. With his arm around me, I helped him walk to his girlfriend's house on Bates Street. From there, we called the ambulance.

This also happened in 1998, my last year of high school. I actually wrote about the incident for an English paper. The assignment was to interview someone in your neighborhood about a startling event. So I decided to interview Shakey about his account of the shooting. I received an A.

To this day, Shakey and I laugh about how quickly he popped up and ran, his jump, why he felt it necessary to jump, and how long his jump was. There was nothing obstructing Shakey's path but a big, long puddle. Why he didn't just run through the puddle is beyond me, beyond both of us. Shakey leapt the entire puddle as though it was just as dangerous as the gunshots. We talk about that leap as though he could have broken the world record for long jump. In my mind, I see Shakey jumping in slow motion, and each time I remember it, his stride becomes longer and longer. I'm glad at least we can laugh about it now.

But a few months later, Brock was stabbed to death. His murder was connected to the attempt at the dice game and the war with Sursum Corda. He had been marked for death, and where we're from, it's hard to move that spot off of you.

That death mark had also been on me, and not only in the many times I've been on the block and guys came through shooting. Once I was told I was actually singled out for an attempt. Someone I knew from Sursum Corda told me the word was they were going to get Slugg. Why? I don't know. It wasn't that I was involved in anything. After the guns came out and Lil' Dennis died, I tried my best to stay neutral. Naming me was just them being angry, wanting to get whomever. It's crazy to me that I could be named. Again, for the most part, we all knew each other. But if a friend could take your life, how hard then is it for an associate? I guess this is nothing new; Cain slew his brother Abel. I just wish it wouldn't happen with such frequency in the hood.

Unknowingly, I was being prepared for a part of the peace work I do today back in my 1st and O days. I found myself in situations where I had to talk my partners out of shooting someone. Had I not intervened, there's no question in my mind their guns would have sparked, and something awful would have happened. Where I'm from, guys didn't raise their guns for show; if they brought their gun up, they were going to use it to destroy. Once, while we were all standing on North Capitol and O, a guy named Smoke from Sursum Corda was walking from the store alongside his mother. Smoke was known for being a thorough guy, meaning he was tough and would bust his gun. Still, I don't know what Smoke was thinking about walking past us like that. Perhaps he felt since he was with his mother, he'd get a pass. I don't know. Giving him a pass is certainly not what my guys were thinking. As soon as my man saw Smoke, he leveled his gun and was about to shoot him. I couldn't let that happen. Not with his mother by his side. She was innocent, not at all involved in the madness. My moral compass back then is not what it is today. I had a street mentality that was buffered by my morality, and this really was the only way that I was effective. I had earned my respect before the guns came out, and I had demonstrated my toughness without one. But when the gun became *the* factor, when guys started saying with pride, "Fighting? We don't do no motherfucking fighting," they didn't need me for protection anymore. I don't want to make it sound like fistfights didn't happen. Being able to fight was still respected, but the gun was used and respected more.

I played the role of an interrupter a number of other times. Once, when I was standing on the corner with Stinka and the rest of the crew, my man Rabbit came through our neighborhood. Rabbit was from Sursum Corda, and as he was walking up, Stinka recognized that and immediately raised his gun, ready to shoot him. Quickly, I talked Stinka down, explaining that Rabbit was coming to see me. Rabbit lived in the Cordas, but like me, he wasn't active in the beef. He and I played on the same basketball team up at Colors. Colors was the playground the neighborhood nicknamed "White and Colored" due to the fact that years before it was one of the first playgrounds in D.C. to be integrated. My generation just called it Colors, maybe because no white people came around anymore. Anyway, playing on the same rec league team there, I got to know Rabbit well.

Sometimes guys in my crew would get mad at me and say, "Slugg, I don't know why you keep trying to save these niggas. They not gon try to save you." They had a point. The war with Sursum Corda was volatile and constant. They would come through shooting at whoever was outside, and Shakey and I were always outside. In my neighborhood, either you stay inside all the time and grow depressed, or go outside and breathe the fresh air, interact with your peers, feel alive, and risk being shot. So we were shot at quite often.

At times, I went from feeling neutral to being livid, thinking, "They not just gon keep coming around here fucking shooting..." But I couldn't kill or order a killing. I feared God, not man. I've never been afraid of another man. I knew I could do whatever he could. That's how I was raised. I just believed in right and wrong. The difference between me and my peers is that I had a true concept of morality and they didn't. What's viewed as wrong to most of society was looked at as right to them in a lot of ways. Still, that sense I had handicapped me in the street. While I'm weighing the rights and the wrongs of a situation, these guys are already busting that hot shit at you.

In my high school years, the police were also a serious threat. In 1997, our neighborhood changed police districts. We went from the 1st district of the Metropolitan Police Department to the 3rd district. From the beginning, the 3rd district sought to set an example that they were a no-nonsense police force. They were, by far, much tougher than the 1st district. As an example of their excessiveness, one day around that time a neighborhood drug addict we called Luge Dooger rushed to our house to notify Kim that she was about to get a parking ticket. Because of his warning, Kim came out in time to move her car and did not receive a ticket. This infuriated the officers who were ticketing. Who knows what ridiculous charge they came up with, but they used it to try to handcuff Luge Dooger.

LD was heavily addicted to crack, but he was still very strong and had just come home from Lorton. He fought back, and the two officers couldn't handle him. LD dropped one of the officers

140

with a punch, prompting his partner to radio "officer down" to the station. The fallen officer got back up, and the two of them continued to struggle with LD. Eventually, the entire block had come out to watch the scuffle. No one else had assaulted the police, but we were yelling for the police officers to leave LD alone. Initially, he had done nothing to warrant that kind of treatment. The backup had come, and with their collective force, they subdued LD. We couldn't stand to see him treated that way over a parking ticket and became louder and more outraged. Nervous about the mood of the crowd, the officers called in a "code red," and in no time what seemed to be the entire 3rd district was on Hanover in full riot gear! This set a precedent. From that day forward, my neighborhood was at odds with the 3rd district.

These were the prime years of my 1st and O days. When you're hanging on the block as much as I did, the police become very familiar with you, and you with the police. Of all the police in the 3rd district, the most feared officer of the group regarded me with great animosity. Officer Ortiz was short and stocky with tattoos all over his arms. He had jet-black hair and wore a thick mustache. We had been accustomed to white police officers in our neighborhood, but Ortiz was one of the first Hispanic officers to come around.

The guy was a rogue cop. He'd plant drugs on people, beat them up without just cause, and take money from crap games, but his greatest influence came in locking guys up. There's no telling how many of my friends Ortiz wrongfully arrested and sent to jail. I wasn't living an illegal life, so he never got me; still, he never gave up trying. He had it out for me. I didn't understand why back then, but now I think it was because of my presence. I also knew my rights and would not be harassed. Sometimes when he and his band of fellow officers came around to shake things up, he'd let everyone else in the crew go and just search me. Other times he'd look at me and tell me if he found a stash it would belong to me. He'd search my car even when I wasn't in it. But being that it was always parked directly in front of the house, Grandma, Aunt Bonnie, and other older women on the block wouldn't stand for it. They'd come to my defense, saying, "That boy ain't doing nothing. Leave him alone." For this, he nicknamed me Mama's Boy.

Ortiz would speak poorly about your family and anything he thought you held dear. He'd say to guys, "That's why your mother's a crack whore." Like a gangster, he told Shakey to never walk on the side of the street he patrolled. Shakey didn't want to get locked up and took the order seriously. It wasn't funny then, but it became another one of those funny moments Shakey and I would look back on.

Ortiz's continuously harassed and humiliated me. I remember so many illegal searches in the summer, palms on a burning hot hood of a car, him looking down my pants, feeling my buttocks, supposedly searching for drugs, whispering in my ear, "I'm going to get you motherfucker," before letting me go, but he didn't move me. I didn't fear him, and he knew it. His focus on me actually saved my friends who *were* involved in criminal activity. Ironically, he'd let them go to bother me. After a while, there were so many complaints about Ortiz's behavior he was removed from our area and placed in another.

In those years, even the events that were the most fun could be the most dangerous. When I was growing up, D.C. was over seventy percent black and go-go music was king. Go-go is to D.C. what jazz is to New Orleans and hip-hop is to New York City—it was our indigenous music, and we loved it. Go-go is a fusion of funk and R&B. It is percussion-driven music, highlighted by horns, keys, and strong vocals that you must experience live to appreciate. Unlike jazz and hip-hop, I believe go-go music didn't spread globally or even very much nationally for this reason. The feeling of the atmosphere at a go-go, the pheromonal heat, the passionate dancing, all present in sync yet still doing your own thing to the beat, the call from the artists and the response from the audience, cannot be captured and played back.

When you went to see a go-go band, we called it going to the go-go. From 1996 to 1999, me and my crew went to the go-go nearly every Friday. Chuck Brown was the godfather of go-go music, and there were many bands such as Rare Essence, Junkyard Band, Lil Benny and the Masters, EU, and Northeast Groovers. But Back Yard was the band for us. Back Yard was for the young, reckless, and aggressive crowd, which was perfect for 1st and O. The leader of that band was Anwan "Big G" Glover, who would later play the part of Slim in HBO's *The Wire*.

Anwan knew that life.

As beautiful as the music was, from the mid-1980s through the 1990s, going to the go-go began to be associated with violence and danger. The go-go was one of the main places my father would try to warn me away from. Many had died or gotten shot at the go-go, but that didn't discourage me from going. The way we saw it, you didn't matter if you did not go. I mattered, so I had to be there, and when I went my presence had to be felt. I inherited my extroversion from my mother, and I'd be all over the go-go, floating and partying as if I were the sole ambassador for the music and the scene.

My crew would travel all around the D.C. area to see Back Yard, or Back as we called them, but my favorite place to see Back Yard was the infamous Black Hole. The Black Hole was especially violent. The venue was in the northwest part of the city off Georgia Avenue, and when you went, you knew gangsters and crews from all over the city would be there. Again, we were the Hanover 1st and O/NCO crew, and we had to make our mark. The security entering the Black Hole was like the checkpoints before boarding a flight at an airport post-September 11th. It was extremely difficult to get a weapon through. There were plenty of fistfights at the Black Hole, though, and I was in my fair share. Still, I also developed some of my best mediating skills there.

Fighting at the go-go really didn't do much for your reputation, which meant everything at the time. Your reputation came and was solidified when the lead person on the microphone

144

acknowledged that your crew was present. As a teenager, I knew some of Back Yard's band members, and they definitely knew my dad. So out of respect, they would "put me on," meaning Big G and Weensy would call out my name and our hood on the mic. Hearing my name and our hood called was the best feeling. It meant I was somebody; I was Lil' Tony Lewis from Hanover. We used to rush to buy the tapes where we were called out, and we'd listen to them over and over, basking in the music and our moment of glory.

By the end of high school, my classmates and good friends Dorjan and Jahmal worked up the courage to go with me to the go-go at the Black Hole. My friend Dave also went with us once or twice. It was an eye-opening experience for them. Dorjan and Jahmal's family weren't affluent, but they were solidly middle class. They were from D.C., but there was a clear distinction from the way they were raised and the way I came up.

I also used to bring my cousin Alan on occasion. At that time, with him being fourteen and yet to hit his growth spurt and me being three years older, I was still taller than him. Alan had a caramel complexion and a distinct birthmark, three dark spots, on his right eye. He was skinny as a kid, but as he got older, he filled out and grew much taller than me. I don't know who I thought I was, but I used to walk through the go-go as if I were untouchable. I'd tell Alan to hold onto the back of my shirt and he would. He held onto my shirt for dear life, trailing me as a baby duck trails his mother. Alan was more like my little brother, and I would never let anything happen to him.

145

Years later, when Alan was old enough to go to the go-go on his own, he got into a police chase coming home from one. He tried to outrun the police and ended up sideswiping a half a block of cars, then crashing and totaling his car. This happened on Benning Road, right in front of the 6th district police station. Thankfully, Alan was all right and nobody else got hurt, but by the time I got to the scene, they had already locked him up. I went into the police station to see how he was doing, but Alan had to go to court the next day, where he was released on his own recognizance.

Another night around this time, Alan was staying with us and had come home from the go-go. I stayed home that time and had a lady friend over at the house with me. In the middle of the night while we were in bed asleep, she stirred, waking me up, and pointed to a shadow in my room. It was Alan. I could see his silhouette in the darkness, but he was just standing there. I asked him what he was doing, but he didn't respond. Then all of a sudden, I hear a whizzing sound. Still half sleep and not concerned, I didn't realize what the sound was until it was too late. When I finally realized what he was doing, Alan had already urinated on my television, my books, and everything else beneath the TV. I screamed at him, "Alan! What the fuck you doing, man?" He just turned to me casually, as though he had not just pissed all over my books, her clothes and shoes, and all over the floor, and said, "Oh, what's up, Ton?" before pivoting and going back to his room. He was sleepwalking and thought he had gone to use the bathroom. I got up immediately, avoiding the big puddle on my floor, and followed him to his room. When I got there, I saw he had a clump of vomit and spit on his pillow that he just laid right down beside. I woke him up and made him clean every bit of it.

Gonzaga is only a few blocks from Hanover, but at the same time, for me, it was another world away. In my junior year, our physics lab overlooked Sursum Corda and Temple Courts. That time was the height of the beef, and many had already died. One day, while doing some work in the lab after school, a classmate and I were gazing out the window at the buildings. This classmate's father happened to be a superstar in the Worldwide Wrestling Federation (now called WWE). As we stared, we were thinking completely different thoughts. He turned to me and said, "Tony, is your neighborhood like what they show in the movies? You know, guys drinking forty-ounce beers, selling drugs, having barbecues..." He didn't mean to be offensive. I could see that in his eyes. Still, the question stung. I looked at him and said, "Not every day," and then walked to a lab table and occupied myself with work.

As I handled my equipment, his question moved all through me, cutting me each time it changed direction. I was a kid and not yet articulate enough to convey the pain, nuance, and complexity of my environment, and he was a kid with no awareness or sensitivity for my culture, though my world was merely blocks away. I've found people either see the hood as a place devoid of hope, or they overestimate the hope to be found there.

My classmates at Gonzaga would invite me over to their homes, but I never accepted their invitations. It's something that I look back on with regret. I was afraid to step outside of my comfort zone. I wasn't nearly as open to newness and difference as I am today. If I could go back and talk to the much younger me, I'd tell myself many things, one being to embrace new positive opportunities, often, no matter how foreign they seem. Tremendous growth comes from new challenges and shared knowledge between those of disparate cultures.

A significant part of my interactions with my classmates out-side of school came from the rides I'd get. Walking home took less than ten minutes, but at the height of our feud with Sursum Corda it wasn't the smart move. So my friends Pierro, Steve, and Glen would often pick me up from school and take me home when school was out.

I didn't really find my stride at Gonzaga until my senior year. Coincidentally, that's when I took my two favorite classes of high school, social justice and philosophy. My most-influential teacher at Gonzaga was an old legendary priest name Father Lucien Longtin. Father Longtin was highly respected and feared. He taught a philosophy class called "Systematic Theology." The class came at a poor time for some of the seniors that were ready to kick their feet up and coast the rest of their way through school. I had never read so much at one time. It was intense, but I enjoyed it. You name the philosopher, and we read something substantial from them. Father Longtin would

148

split up the class each day, and you had to debate the other side using the reading you did for homework. You never knew which side you were going to be on; you had to either attack or defend the material. I excelled in that class. I loved it. I loved the way he taught it. It was about challenging us to think independently while showing us the importance of faith and the responsibility to help those around us.

Father Longtin's class was the perfect complement to my social justice class, which was taught by a teacher named Mr. Turner. I remember being in Mr. Turner's class one day, and the topic of discussion centered on communities like Hanover. Mr. Turner talked about how important it was for those who come from a privileged background to give of their time and resources. I raised my hand and asked Mr. Turner what about if you come from one of those neighborhoods. He responded saying no matter how little you have, you can still give.

I graduated from Gonzaga in June of 1998. The ceremony was held in the sanctuary of our school's church, St. Aloysius. The soon-to-be graduates sat in the pews together, and in the same long rows family, friends, and other guests sat in close proximity to us. My mother, with Aunt Bonnie and Grandma beside her, sat in my same pew only a few feet away from me. Mom was acting up a bit during the ceremony, but the moments right before my name was called she grew still and quiet. I'll never forget: my name was called right after Charles Lexy Lewis. When I heard my name, I stood up to receive my diploma and heard my mother say, "Yes!" It came out like a deep exhale,

149

from the past where the dream was first formed inside of her.

Much was built into my mother's exclamation and that moment. There were many times when I didn't think I'd make it through that place and to that day. Aside from the rigor of the academics and social dynamics at Gonzaga, all that was happening to me around Hanover could have taken me out at any time. But I had made it. After I received my diploma, I sat back down and flashed a big smile in the direction of the three closest women to me in the world. All three of them had a big hand in my success, and sitting there, I felt like there wasn't anything in the world that I could not do.

Dangerous Ambivalence

Father Longtin sent me a handwritten note that summer, a month or so after graduation. In it, he said that the sky was the limit and he encouraged me to become a lawyer based on my ability to debate. The letter came as a complete surprise, and I was touched by it. None of the classmates with whom I spoke later said he ever sent them anything like that. While Father Longtin's note was empowering, it came at a time that I didn't really know what I wanted to do. It was true, in graduating from Gonzaga I felt there was nothing I couldn't do. But what was I going to do? I didn't know. I was accepted to Howard University, but the only reason I applied is because everyone at Gonzaga went to college, so I went to college. But after being at Howard for only a week, I dropped out. I felt no sense of purpose there, so I returned to Hanover and to the corner of 1st and O. I didn't feel as whole hanging on the block as I used to feel, but at least I felt something.

My neighbors started watching me very closely when I left Howard. What was I going to do? All of them knew the avenue of drug dealing was a path I could take because not only did I have the legacy, but also the capability. I knew how to move, was a bona-fide member of 1st and O, and carried myself like a general. So after high school, the talk about me, specifically by the elders, started to change. They sensed the inevitable. To many of them, I had the look of someone who had already joined the ranks. The way my crew responded to me led them to believe *something* had to be going on.

Grandma heard all the chatter, and one day sat me down to say I was hanging on the block too much. She insisted that I do something more with myself. If Howard wasn't right, what about the University of the District of Columbia? "Dee Dee went to UDC..."

But after dropping out, going back to school was the farthest thing from my mind. It wasn't for me. Still, I couldn't escape Grandma's eye—the way she looked at me—not only in the moment she sat me down, but in every waking moment thereafter. She was worried about me, and she should have been.

In January of 1999, I enrolled at UDC out of respect for Grandma's wishes. The following summer, for the same reasons our neighbors were in Grandma's ear, a local hustler offered me two kilograms of cocaine to sell. In his mind, it was a promotion. Given the leadership and presence he observed, he figured the offer would be mutually beneficial, not unlike the proposition Cornell Jones pitched to my father many years before. My considering the offer might seem strange given how close I was to my father's incarceration. But, more often than not, that kind of logic doesn't work in the hood. Jay-Z has a line in "Allure" from *The Black Album* that explains this common scenario in my community perfectly. He raps about footprints left in the ghetto and how, without words being exchanged, a little brother will follow a big brother into crime. The little brother follows the big brother despite knowing how it's very likely going to end. He's seen the fate of his big brother, yet he proceeds and progresses to play the same role. Before I heard the lyrics, I lived them. Instead of my brother hustling, it was my father. The only difference is I didn't play; I rejected the offer, but this would not be a turning point. I still had a lot of growing to do.

I was in school, but still hanging on the block in all my free time. Determined to get me off the corner, Grandma teamed up with Aunt Bonnie, and the two of them contacted a friend of my father's named Fat Rob. Rob worked as a roving leader, which was an outreach position for the city. I wasn't old enough or experienced enough to be a roving leader, but Rob helped me to become a junior roving leader. It was my first job and the beginning of the work I do today. But back then, even as my eyes were being opened and seeds were being planted for the life I lead now, I existed in contradiction. As I took college courses and worked as an outreach worker, I still fully embraced the days and ways of 1st and O, which could only lead to death. This was demonstrated again right before me the winter after I started at UDC.

Standing on the porch with Grandma and Shakey one day, the three of us watched in horror as a hit man dressed in all black, wearing black sunglasses, calmly approached an idling car and shot its only occupant, the driver, dead. The driver was a guy named Carlos. He was wearing the Los Angeles Lakers Avirex jacket that I had recently complimented him on, and now I was watching him die in it.

Carlos wasn't from Hanover or the surrounding area, but he used to come around our way a lot to spend time with his girlfriend, Hopey, who lived on our block. We all knew Carlos was involved in the streets, but none of us standing there could have imagined we'd watch him be executed. Especially not in that way. It was no drive-by shooting or a wild neighborhood shooter walking up; it was a professional hit: cold, calculated, and precise.

Grandma screamed, "No! No! No!" as we watched the assassin's first bullets strike Carlos. Instinctively, he tried driving off, but the shots had mortally wounded him and he ended up losing control of the car. It coasted and crashed not too far up the block from where we were still standing. Jogging to finish the job, the hit man turned and looked at us. It was a terrifying glance. Would he turn the gun on us?

He didn't. Instead, he kept jogging to the stopped car, and upon reaching it, he shot Carlos a number of more times before calmly escaping the scene.

Once the hit man was out of sight, me and Shakey went to the car to see about Carlos, knowing full well what we'd find when we got there.

About four months after Carlos was killed, I started my job as a junior roving leader. One of my first assignments in the position was being a part of the skate mobile team. For three

154

summers, beginning in 2000, I rode to the toughest neighbor-hoods in the city in an old utility truck (like that of the electric company) with my mentors, James and Darby. James was a Southeast D.C. guy who was a former athlete and college graduate. Darby was a reformed street dude, now living on the straight and narrow path and trying to do the right thing. James had played on a championship Dunbar High School basketball team. He wore glasses, a light beard, and got his hair cut week-ly, always keeping himself neat. Darby was short and smooth. He was a sharp dresser with a swagger from the 1980s. He had straight hair, like a Native American's, that he always brushed and kept short. Both were at least ten years older than me, but I was used to being around older guys.

The skate mobile had only two front seats and no air condi-tioning. As we rode, I sat between James and Darby in a fold-up chair. Obviously, this was a serious safety risk, but I didn't care. I was instead too excited about the work. In the summer heat, starting at 8:00 a.m., we would go out on our prepared route and work until 4:30 p.m. We made about four stops a day. Our schedule was prepared by the roving leader office, which sent us daily to recreation centers in communities that were consid-ered hot spots or high-crime areas. We would service the summer camps at these rec centers. Designating open concrete areas like basketball courts or even sometimes blocked-off streets, we'd take the cones out of the skate mobile and set up a perimeter. Then we'd take out our generator, radio, and big speaker and crank up the good vibes by booming go-go music.

The speaker was powerful, so our music filled the air to the surrounding areas. It became our calling card, like the friendly music of the ice cream man. Although we weren't selling sweet treats, we were handing out roller skates, roller blades, and razor scooters for the children to enjoy. On occasion, we ventured into affluent neighborhoods with the same service, and for the most part, whether rich or poor, the kids loved it.

Mostly children from the ages of seven to thirteen would take advantage of our skate mobile service. In a good many of the neighborhoods we were strangers. Having no ties taught us to sharpen our outreach skills and better engage the parents and youth of the community. Still, we did have a few tense moments. We had to be careful and ever vigilant when entering neighborhoods where we had no personal ties. A few times, there were young men on the block who felt like our services brought too much attention to them. We were making too much noise or were making the block "hot," and they'd not so politely tell us to leave. I never took it personally, but James would. He'd get righteously indignant, talking this and that about the good of the service. But those guys weren't trying to hear that. I knew them and in a sense was once them, though I would have never turned away something positive from my community. While James fumed, I'd be looking at him like, "Man, these dudes ain't playing. And I'm not about to die over no skates." Once while we were setting up at Benning Park, things almost got out of hand. I had to really calm James down and redirect his energy so we could get out of there in one

156

piece. Some battles just aren't worth fighting, even when you're right.

A roving leader's role is to be an all-day presence in a child's life. We worked in the school during the day and in the community in the evening. Our hours were from about 12 p.m. to 8 p.m. We were assigned to children that were having difficulty with behavior in school and in their communities. One of my first outreach opportunities as a junior roving leader was working with Darby in the Potomac Gardens housing projects. Darby had already established relationships with many of the children from working in their elementary and junior high schools. After school, Darby and I would walk the courtyards of Potomac Gardens. We'd make home visits and meet the children's mothers. Very rarely was there a father in the home. Darby would tell me never to get romantically involved with the mothers. To some this might seem obvious, but children's advocacy, enrichment, and educational programs are often poisoned by adult workers' lack of integrity and professionalism.

One of our great strengths in working in Potomac Gardens was that we knew some of the residents. I knew some personally, and Darby had made his inroads. One of those connections was with a guy named Omar. Omar was a highly respected street dude in that community who in turn respected Darby's past. Once we got his stamp of approval, we moved freely and without provocation, and, over time, the community began to treat us like family. One of the things that various non-profit organizations and advocacy programs get wrong is not making a solid, genuine connection to some respected person of the community. This may seem like common sense, but often people mistake money, resources, and token efforts to connect with the community as enough to effect real change. Nothing will change until there's trust built. A good way to expedite the building of that trust is by establishing and maintaining a genuine connection to a well-respected member of the community.

The first time I spoke publicly was at the behest of James. He had coordinated a Father's Day event at Sharpe Elementary School. The goal was to get as many father and son groups as we could. About thirty fathers and sons showed up. Once the crowd settled and James made his remarks, it was my turn to speak. Nervously, I opened my mouth and, to my surprise, didn't sound that bad. I encouraged the fathers to be active participants in their sons' lives. I expressed to them that I had a better relationship with my father who was doing life in prison than many men from our communities had with their sons in freedom. Knowing that a big part of the problem with absent fathers in the hood was due to mass incarceration, I asked them not to take chances with their freedom. "Don't get taken. Your sons and daughters need you."

I was doing the best I could to follow my own advice, but in the hood, when you're really a part of the community, you have to work extremely hard to stay away from trouble.

One day I walked from Hanover to meet up with my friends

Damon and Aaron. At this point of my life, we were together all the time. The three of us had plans to drive to Mazza Gallerie to get some clothes for the club later that evening. I won big gambling the night before, so I also wanted to get a Techno Marine watch.

As I approached, I saw that Aaron's big cousin was with them. I shake up with everyone, and we all start talking about the basketball player Allen Iverson. It's 2001, and A.I.'s on a tear. Later that year he'd be named the N.B.A.'s most valuable player. He's not from the D.C. area, but he's a Hoya and from the hood; he's our man. A little man, dominating in a big man's game with otherworldly talent and toughness. When he wins, we win. No other player embodied the essence of our generation more...

Wait. Who's this? The Jump Outs? They've appeared out of nowhere. How many of them are there? One, two, three, four... They're rounding the four of us up. They make us turn around and face the building we're standing next to, but they don't handcuff us. *Am I being arrested? I didn't do anything.* I look over my shoulder. These detectives move differently. They're extremely confident and efficient. They're not saying much, going in my pocket and pulling out my I.D. Now, they're pulling my bank roll out of my sock. *Man, they're going to take my money.* But they don't. They write something down and hand the money back to me. *What the hell is going on?* They take Damon's keys and go straight for the trunk of a car. I don't recognize the car. *What are they looking for?* They pull a book

159

bag out of the trunk. *Man, I hope there ain't no drugs in that bag. Please, don't let there be no drugs in that bag.* "Ah hah," one of them says, "What do we have here?" He's unzipped the bag and instead of bricks of cocaine there are bundles of money. Money's better. I'm relieved. But I still don't know what's going on. The officers take the bag and let us all go. What just happened? No one is talking. My guys know something, but they're not saying anything. I don't think they know exactly what happened either.

A month or so passed and I got my answer. A certified letter from the United States Justice Department came to my home addressed to me. In it was an affidavit from the U.S. Attorney's office, a complaint for forfeiture. Those were not Metropolitan police officers who had apprehended us. They were the F.B.I. The book bag they removed from the trunk had $31,000 in it. The affidavit went on to explain how the bag got in the trunk, which all happened before I walked up, and involved Aaron's cousin, Aaron, and Damon. Then it went on to detail how the agents searched the trunk and seized the bag. The affidavit concluded with the following: "WHEREFORE, the United States prays that due process issue to enforce the forfeiture of the defendant currency and that due notice be given to all interested parties to appear and show cause why said forfeiture should not be adjudged."

Holding this document in my hands and reading it sent chills through me. This was the *F.B.I.* They don't look to get lucky. When they come for you, they have you. I understood this better than most, and I immediately thought about my father and all his admonishments. I couldn't tell him about this. How could I be so stupid, allowing myself to be caught up in this shit? I wasn't involved in the business of it. Damon wasn't either. His girlfriend's car was just holding the money for a moment before another car came. Aaron's cousin didn't feel comfortable standing outside with that amount of money. The F.B.I. agents knew that. The affidavit was mailed to me because I was there for the seizure, but I was not mentioned by name in the official document as Damon, Aaron, and Aaron's cousin were. Still, it was mailed to me. Were they watching me too? Had they made the connection to my father? And why didn't Aaron tell me that he was in the life? I was upset at him for that. Our relationship wouldn't have changed much, but I had the right to know. We were together almost every day, and his actions affected me. I had been under the impression he was like me. At one time he was. I knew what his cousin did, but Aaron never told me he was working with him.

Eventually, Aaron's cousin received thirty years for that case. Aaron would do jail time for it too. It seemed no matter where I turned, trouble was waiting for me, trying to catch me in its jaws. Even my ex-girlfriend, Tracie, who used to keep me off the streets—though being with her family kept me around that element—became, in an instant, a part of the trap.

Tracie and I were extremely close in our late teens. I guess you could call us sweethearts. But at first she didn't want me. It took another girl, Christina, having me before Tracie wanted me. Christina was good friends with a girl named Donyale who lived on Hanover. Donyale's family was out of place on our block. She lived in a two-parent household, and both parents were professionals. Mr. Willis, Donyale's stepfather, was the only man I ever saw leave the block to work a job every day. Anyway, Donyale, Christina, and Tracie went to Georgetown Visitation, which is a private school and sister school to Gonzaga.

Christina would visit Donyale on Hanover and be received like a superstar. A mixture of Spanish and Black, she was light-skinned and had long, curly hair, full lips, and a beautiful body. She turned our hood out. And the fact that she also had a car took her status to an even higher level. She lived in a nice neighborhood uptown with her mother and stepfather. Her mother worked for the World Bank and her father was a lawyer. We didn't usually see her kind around my way. When she'd come by, guys would literally stand in line to try to talk to her. They'd take turns, one at a time, trying to make a go at her. They tried to get her attention by showing off, making fun of one another, and other displays intended to impress. I'd be around, but I would never say anything. I couldn't see myself participating in that nonsense.

Christina was around again one day as I was walking to B&V corner store. She flagged me down, saying, "Hey, can you come here for a second?"

"Me?" I thought. When I walked over to her, she asked me why I never spoke. I told her I didn't speak because I didn't know her. Then I quickly added I had never gotten the chance to know her because every time she came around, the whole hood was in her face. She smiled, we exchanged names, and I kept moving. Of course, all the homies wanted to know what was said between us, but I didn't let on. I played it cool.

The next day we were all gambling in the alley. It was my turn to shoot when Christina came to the entrance of the alley and called to me. Everyone looked up, and all twenty-something of the homies surrounding me started hating. Here I was winning the game *and* being chosen by one of the finest girls we had ever seen. I felt like the man! I didn't walk over to her right away though. I acknowledged her and took my turn shooting the dice. When I crapped out, I got up and walked over to her. She asked if I wanted to go to the mall with her. Did I!

When she came back around with her car, I felt all the eyes on me. As I stepped in, before getting my other leg into the car, I looked over my shoulder, smiled, and nodded to the whole crew. They were mad with envy.

Christina and I had a good time at the mall, but she made me nervous. I didn't know her angle. Why was she taking such an interest in me? About a week later, she'd drive me away in her car again, but the second time came after I'd been battling in the street. I had no idea Christina had been there to see it.

A guy named Coz used to hustle in our neighborhood despite not being from there. I was still trying to get with Tracie and had just returned to Hanover from seeing her when I heard some commotion. I was on my bicycle, and as I pedaled down

163

the block closer to my house, I saw that it was Coz making all the noise. He was enraged. Someone had stolen his stash—120 rocks, he proclaimed. As I listened, he started saying he was going to kill everybody on the block, my block. Now, I was seventeen and Coz was in his mid-twenties, but I didn't care. It was a warm summer night, and Grandma and other families from Hanover were outside enjoying the weather. I stepped off the bike and asked him to clarify who he was talking about. He snapped at me, telling me to mind my "motherfucking business." We exchanged a few more words, and before I know it, we're in the middle of the street with our guards up. I swing first and catch him with a combination of punches. He staggers and swings back. I bob and weave that and catch him with a hook that drops him but doesn't knock him out. When he pops up to run, I chase him and hit him from behind, which makes him fall again. I begin to stomp him, and Jon-Jon—who I had known since birth and who had moved back to Hanover after living in Maryland —joined me in the stomping until people pulled us off of him.

Afterwards, the word got around fast about what had happened. I was on the phone in my house when Christina walked in. I don't know who let her in and, again, I didn't even know she was there to see it. But in the moment I didn't really care about all of that. She asked me to ride with her, saying I needed to get away for a minute. In my mind I was thinking, "This girl is *mean*." My nervousness went away.

Tracie was upset when she found out I was dating Christina.

She saw a bit of betrayal in it, reminding me that Christina had driven her to Hanover to see me sometime before. But Tracie wasn't interested in me then. Now she was. And, at some point, I had to make a choice. Christina was gorgeous, and she encouraged me in areas that didn't much interest me. It was she who completed my SAT waiver form and practically forced me to take the test. Still, I chose Tracie because we had a lot more in common. I had never been more comfortable around any other female. With us, things were just understood. We were young, in love, and together all the time.

My family and Tracie's family were close, so she and I had known each other for years. Tracie was like the female me. Both of us had gone to Catholic schools our entire lives, and her father, Folks, was a prominent hustler like my father. From 1997—which is the year Tracie and I started dating seriously— until 2001, I spent a lot of time around Tracie's father.

I never saw my father with drugs, but with Folks I did. Folks didn't live with Tracie and her mother, but he'd come by a lot. Folks was very light skinned and a big dude, about 6'2", 280 pounds solid. Often, he'd prepare the cocaine at their house. I remember the crack aroma being so thick. He and I used to play dominoes as he cooked the bricks of coke in the microwave. When he wasn't there and I was just relaxing with Tracie over at her house, I'd be extra vigilant when warming up my food in the microwave, praying no crack residue seeped into my plate.

Folks treated me like a son. He would give me money and expose me to new things as I traveled often with Tracie and the family. As a Christmas present, he also financed my final trip to see my father in California. That was 1999, and it was the only time of the three trips that I was able to go alone to see my father.

Tracie and I broke up during her junior year of college. She went to LaSalle University in Philadelphia, and our relationship couldn't survive the distance. But we were good friends and would still be intimate on occasion. During the winter holiday break of 2001, she and I spoke frequently. I called her on New Year's Eve, and we agreed that we would see each other that night. She said she'd come around Hanover.

Tracie brought the New Year in at a club called the D.C. Tunnel, and I celebrated it over at her cousin Aaron's house. I left Aaron's at about 3 a.m. and headed to Hanover. Before I arrived home, Tracie and I had spoken on the telephone. She said she was on her way home too and would be by to see me soon. I called back about a half an hour later when she hadn't shown up yet. She told me that she was at home but was having some car trouble. In all the time we were together, I had never announced that I was coming over. I always just showed up, and Tracie only lived five minutes away, so I decided to go pick her up.

I took Grandma's Lincoln, and as I approached Tracie's house, I saw two of her girlfriends sitting in a car. I blew the horn at them and parked. I got out of the car and knocked on the door; the door opened slowly with the rapping of my fist, so

I entered. The first thing I saw was Tracie and a 6'4" stranger. I was surprised, and I go from excited to see her to being a bit disturbed. I thought we agreed that we were going to see each other. I thought she was on her way. What about the car trouble? But I'm cool. I was taught to never fight over a female, and I couldn't be farther from that emotion. I politely asked Tracie if I could speak with her in private, and the guy says, "Anything you have to say to her you can say right here." Oh, yeah? In the same moment, Tracie's mother comes down the stairs and says, "Tony, don't come over here with that." The mixture of it all had me confused, so without saying a word I walk out, get back in my car, and head home.

Back at home and in bed, I was not really mad—just a bit shocked and disappointed in Tracie. Why didn't she just tell me she wanted to see another guy? We weren't boyfriend and girlfriend anymore. Being upfront with me would have been nothing. My phone rang. I picked it up and heard the voice of the 6'4" guy. He called me by name, saying, "Tony...it ain't like that."

"I don't know you, and I don't know why you're calling my phone," I said. "Shorty's not be trusted, so don't wife her." I hung up on him and immediately called Tracie. She picked up, and I screamed at her and asked her what her problem is. But she seems to be in some kind of trance. I hung up. Then the guy called my phone again, saying they were on the way to my house.

"Stop hitting my phone, champ!" I yelled.

Minutes later, the guy called back.

They were outside.

It was twenty degrees. But I go outside in shorts, Timberland boots, and no shirt. Mad as hell, I just popped right out of bed, threw my shoes on, and went out the door. *What's Tracie doing bringing him to my house?* It was 4:30 a.m. and no one was outside on the block. I approached Tracie's car. There was another guy in the back seat, and Tracie was in the passenger seat. I had nothing on me, but they probably did. They were in a car on New Year's Eve, a time when virtually everyone in the hood is strapped. This all occurred to me in the moment, but I didn't care. I had to find out what was going on with Tracie. How could she be one of the closest people to me and at the same time be intentionally putting my life in danger? Bringing these dudes to my home with my mother and grandmother inside? Given all that I had seen, all the setups, my senses were going crazy. My instincts were telling me this could be deadly, and for what?

But I kept moving forward to find an answer.

I walked to Tracie's side of the car and begin cursing her out and questioning her at the same time. She didn't respond. She just sat there looking dumbfounded. I continued to spew profanities at her, and the 6'4" guy said, "Watch how you talk to her."

I had been ignoring his entire existence up until that point, but the boldness of his tone made me think he definitely had a weapon. Coming to my senses again, I turned and walked away.

168

But 6'4" got out of the car and followed me. I turned and told him to go on, to stop following me, but as I turned to walk again, he was still on my heels, saying, "Tony, let me holla at you."

And I just reacted. Before you kill me, you're going to feel my wrath. I whipped around and just started punishing his ass. I'm a wild man, out of my mind, but my fists are crisp, landing a flurry of blows to his face, overwhelming him. Tracie ran into the fray, screaming at me to stop. I wheeled and hit her! And I didn't feel sorry. They were the enemy. And another one came for me. The guy from the back seat jumped out of the car and attempted to double-team me. But I was too sharp, and now both of them were receiving my blows. They couldn't beat me, so they stopped fighting and went to the trash can, grabbing empty forty-ounce beer bottles. They the bottles on the ground and prepared to stab me. Immediately, I started picking up bricks from the front yard and fired them like fastballs. Grandma was outside by then. She had a stick in her hand, coming to my aid, saying, "Y'all better leave my grandson alone, goddammit!"

Strangely, through all the fighting, I was untouched. Tracie jumped in the car and drove it closer to our house. I fired a brick at her. It was mayhem. I run to grab the metal shovel in our doorway, but Mom was downstairs by then and she held onto me. They took this opportunity to leave, but as they did, they threw a brick through Grandma's car window.

They were gone, but now they had to die. My neighbors had

called the police, and when they arrived, I told them I didn't know what happened. But in my mind I was plotting revenge. I was on fire. They had violated the sanctity of my home, so death to them all. Alan, Shakey, Will, Damon, and Aaron were all over. They knew the look I had in my eye. They knew what had to be done. Not only had Tracie's friends endangered my family, they had an advantage. Now they knew where I lived.

Aaron and Damon left. Shakey, Will, and I armed ourselves and waited in the front room for retaliation. They were all going to pay. Tracie had to pay. As I waited, my mind grew darker. I thought, "I know the security code to Tracie's house."

The retaliation we were anticipating did not come. My friends left and I fell asleep, dreaming of revenge.

The next morning my father called. The word had gotten to him, and he was furious. Quickly, connections were made. The dad of 6'4" knew my dad, and of course we knew everyone in Tracie's family, but I didn't care. I didn't want or need my father's assistance. Then I thought about Folks, Tracie's father, and all he had done for me. I was still terribly upset and disappointed in Tracie, but I knew what she meant to Folks, and I knew if something happened to any of them, I was going to jail. Grandma begged me to leave it all alone, and as my anger subsided, I began to reflect on all that had happened that night along with my role in it.

It was the only time I had ever held a gun with the true conviction to kill someone. But it was just a fight, a fight that might not have been necessary. If they wanted to kill me, they would have killed me. Why break beer bottles? Going to the car and getting their weapons would have been easier. I had seen that move done many times, and as a byproduct I'd been affected. I was just beginning to work in the community and was taking courses at UDC and was supposed to be getting better, not worse. But all those years hanging on the block had warped my mentality. No love. No mercy. No discussion. Just react and kill or be killed. But there were more peaceful ways of resolving things. I knew that. I often had played the peacemaker in my neighborhood, and now I had just begun to do it in other neighborhoods.

If I were again put in a similar situation, how would I react? And how do I prevent myself from getting into the type of situations where I might be forced to react? A few months later, I'd be involved in a confrontation that put these questions right back to the forefront of my mind.

I had to go to class, but the breaks between college courses still allowed me time to hang on the block. One weekday afternoon, a few of us from the crew were hanging by the corner store. My man Glingo walks inside the store to buy something, and after him walks in a guy we had never seen before. He was tall and looked powerfully built, as though he had done some significant years in prison and had gotten the maximum usage from the yard. He must have felt like a bad man because when Abraham, the store's Eritrean clerk, re-turned Glingo's change under the glass, the big guy snatched it and said, "This my change." Glingo smiled and walked out the store.

The big guy had just made a terrible mistake. He may have been a lion, but alone he couldn't withstand the pack of hyenas waiting for him outside. And as soon as he stepped a foot out of the store, the pack pounced on him. I gave him a couple of vicious body blows that buckled him. The rest of the crew was hitting him up top as he tried to fend them off. When I saw they drew blood from the guy's head, I stepped back. I watched as they beat him until he had collapsed on the ground, unmoving.

I left and went to class with the man in that condition. While there, all I could think about was whether the man were dead or alive. After beating him savagely, no one had checked to see if he was still breathing. My crew didn't care if he was alive, only that the man deserved what he got. But did he deserve that? I was sitting in the back of the classroom thinking I could be an accessory to murder. Fortunately, the man did not die. But I still hadn't learned. I went right back to hanging on the block and falling right back into dangerous situation after dangerous situation. Finally, a couple of years later, something happened that made me step back and truly evaluate how I was living.

My big homie from around the way, MG, had just come home from Lorton, a prison built exclusively for D.C. When it was functional, Lorton was known for its groundbreaking prisoner rehabilitation programs. However, in the eighties and nineties, it became overcrowded and gained a more notorious reputation. MG was there during the notorious years.

A group of us were outside, and MG was a little intoxicated, happy to be free. And he started talking tough, saying, "We were roughing shit off down Lorton...stabbing niggas." I guess he felt his age, spending time in prison, and the way he spent the time gave him status and respect years before it should have. So he started trying to school some of the younger guys who were out there. Then he got condescending, saying, "Y'all young niggas couldn't make it down youth center," questioning their toughness. One of the younger guys, named JJ, who was my homie Bobby's little brother, took offense, saying, "This ain't youth center." Now, MG and JJ were separated by about a decade, and not seeing JJ as any kind of threat, MG got aggressive. "What you say, youngin'? You better stop playing with me."

JJ immediately pulled out his gun and replied, "Nigga, I ain't playing with you..."

He wasn't. MG had been in. He didn't know what was happening outside. Things had changed. MG didn't know what I knew about JJ. JJ was about gunplay. So I immediately jumped up and put myself between them. I was facing JJ, who was pointing the gun at MG, intending to blast. I said, "Hold up, y'all not gon do this out here."

JJ was ready to pull the trigger. He had that wild look in his eye. He and I were dancing. He kept saying to me, "Get out the way, Sluggo. Get out the way." Eventually, I convinced JJ to put down the gun and explained to MG that he had to let it go. There was no moralizing in situations like that. Morals had no

173

place. JJ respected me, but he could have just as easily snapped and squeezed the trigger, killing me and MG. I would have died out there, and for what? Why did these situations keep happening?

I didn't have the luxury of being irresponsible in my late teens and early twenties and still look forward to a successful adult life. In fact, my life and all that I looked forward to could be taken in an instant. Why was I playing around? There were so many examples. I knew where I was from, and I knew what happened there. For young people, the freedom to err and bounce back depends on the security and resources one backing them. There are some who have great safety nets to fall back on, and there are those with no net. My crew and I had no net. Yet, we lived most recklessly. Those years commonly accepted for irresponsibility in other cultures are so very critical where I come from. It's the time where too often young men's lives are changed indelibly. All that I had experienced since starting at UDC and ending with JJ and MG finally grabbed my attention as nothing else had before. It woke me up. If I could not change my habitat, I had to change my habits. I could no longer hang on the block. I lived there, but I did not have to live in the way that I always had. I had very positive things going for myself. I had to be strong enough to break old habits and be open and disciplined enough to create and maintain newer, healthier ones. And so I did.

But it wasn't easy, and it didn't happen overnight. On through my mid-twenties, I was very much a work in progress. I kept my promise of not hanging on the block, but while partying I did get into a few more altercations, though they were nothing like the beef I had been a part of on the street. And over time I learned how to control my reactions even in tense social situations. If I were in the nightclub or a party and I saw that tensions were rising, I'd just leave.

Given where I'm from, one of the things that was very hard for me was to separate myself from my crew. They were my brothers and had been there for me through it all, but we were headed in different directions. Being with them for significant periods of time meant being caught on their path, and I could no longer do that. Given this, my social life began to suffer. Who could I hang out with? Within the social and professional world that I was entering, I was an alien. Who else had seen the things I'd seen and survived without a criminal record and the reckoning that comes with being a part of that life?

My good friend, PT, faced the same problem. We both had a love affair shooting dice, and we'd be at the crap games together. But around the same time he and I both recognized what was at stake even when we were only infrequently involved. One night we were out together playing craps when the police came and broke up the game. PT and I moved to make a quick escape, but a couple police officers started chasing us on foot. Now, here I was a roving leader and PT an engineer working at an engineering firm, and we were running away from the police. After we had evaded them, we kind of looked at each other, laughing like, "Man, what are we doing?" We laughed because a part of it was fun and brought us back to our younger days, but really it wasn't funny. Nothing was funny about the risk we were taking. We had come so far and we had to move on completely. We had to stop.

PT's father, Pernell, was part of the old hierarchy on Hanover and is one of my father's closest friends. He went to prison right after Cornell Jones did and came home in 1993. While PT's father was away, his mother kept him active in Boy Scouts, in church, and other extracurricular activities to keep him off the street. PT was from the street and knew the streets, but he wasn't on them as heavy as I was in our teenage years. His father coming home during PT's early teens made all the difference. Like my father, Pernell had hustled to provide a better life for his family. He was a family man, and since that life had taken him away from his family, he didn't return to it when he came home. So PT then had both of his parents playing an active role in his life. Growing up, I used to really admire their family. They reminded me of something I once had.

My relationship with PT became increasingly more important as I began to change my life. The same goes for my cousin Rodney. Rodney is a product of southeast Washington D.C. who went on and graduated from Harvard University. Rodney and I are distant cousins, but close enough that we knew of each other growing up. Once, our families took a trip to Florida together when we were around the ages of eight and nine years old. He and his twin brother, Ronnie, also went to Gonzaga with me for a year before transferring to the Bullis

Academy in Potomac, Maryland. Still, we hardly spoke while we were in high school together. The twins were a year ahead of me, and with so much going on in my life we were practically strangers.

Rodney and I reconnected as I searched for new social outlets and started opening to the possibility of new friends and relationships. Eventually, he and I would become very good friends. Our relationship exposed me to new worlds and new ways of thinking, but things would have gone differently had I not changed my view. Very early in our relationship, while we were both still in college, Rodney asked me to come visit him at Harvard. At the time I thought it was a ridiculous suggestion and refused his invitation. "Ain't nothing happening up there," I said to myself, "why would I want to visit there?" Now, I badly wish I had gone. What an eye-opening experience it would have been. But back then I was a closed-minded kid who, despite my travels with my father and others, remained primarily within a three-block radius. That was my world and, unfortunately, that was all I wanted to know.

Coming from a tough circumstance, the two worst things for one to go without are hope and a healthy curiosity about ways of living beyond your sight.

My rededication to formal education is one of the things that helped me during my transition. I had been taking courses at UDC for few years and was steadily working toward my degree while not changing much about myself personally. As a result, in those years I didn't benefit as much from my education as I could have. But when I began taking my growth and change seriously, I began to hear and see my learning at the college differently. UDC is a city college, and there are a lot of adults with families and jobs who attend. I took the majority of my classes during the timeslots that worked best for these kinds of students, and I often was, by far, the youngest person in the room. From the start, these older students would encourage me: "Young man, you're doing the right thing. Stay with it." In those years that I spent hanging on the block, I really didn't hear them. But as my perspective changed, being in their presence began to inspire me. I saw the focus and determination in their eyes. Speaking with them about their lives, I began to understand the true value of education. I never quite understood its practicality until I spent time with my classmates at UDC. Their work was purposeful. Each day that they came to class ready to work was a step closer to a better life for them and their families. I adopted their perspective and began to think seriously about how I'd like to use my education.

I had a number of good professors at UDC, but the one that had the greatest impact on me was Raja Helou. I took three different courses with Professor Helou, including a class called "The District of Columbia." Professor Helou was a passionate advocate for the poor. With his keen knowledge of history and socio-economics, he had the rare gift of both challenging and engaging his students. Sitting in his classroom, you felt as though he cared about you and the cultivation of your mind. Eventually, I patterned my teaching style a lot after his.

Professor Helou's District of Columbia course focused on D.C. beginning with the time of home rule in the 1970s. It covered the unique dynamics of us being a federal city, our budget, lack of complete autonomy and representation in Congress, and the way the city was run. In the class, we discussed where the city was headed, its politics and culture, and what people working with the poor and underserved would have to do in D.C. to be most effective.

One of the required readings for this course was a book called *Dream City* by Tom Sherwood and Harry Jaffe. It's a D.C. book written with a specific focus on the political lifespan of Marion Barry. Chapter eleven of *Dream City* is crudely titled "Crack Attack." The chapter opens with the promise that it would center on Rayful, which it did, but it also did much more. For not only did it discuss Rayful in detail, it also mentioned Cornell, my father, and me. Reading with the most critical eyes, I found some things to be accurate and other parts to be false. Then I came upon the following passage:

In early 1987, Edmond phoned Alta Rae Zanville.

"You want to go to the Sugar Ray Leonard fight?" he asked. "We're going to Las Vegas. I got an extra ticket. Why don't you come on?"

Zanville said sure and joined the party of ten, including his father, Big Ray; his mother, Bootsie; Columbus "Little Nut" Daniels, an enforcer; Edmond's partner, Tony Lewis; a cousin named Little Frank; and a few others. Lewis brought three children: his son and two nephews. They flew first class and drove around Vegas in a white stretch limousine...Edmond's entourage caught the eye of Melvin Butler, a roving cocaine salesman from the Crips street gang in Los Angeles. The Crips dealt directly with Colombian importers and acted as middlemen in the cocaine distribution system in Los Angeles...Butler checked out Edmond and recognized that he could be a conduit to the lucrative Washington market. Butler introduced Edmond and Lewis to Brian "Waterhead Bo" Bennett, the Crips member who dealt directly with a Columbian supplier, Mario Ernesto Villabona-Alvarado...Edmond was to become one of their best customers.

I was not prepared to read these words. I was there! My seven-year-old self glared back at me from a homework assignment. The book's scant description of the event triggered a visceral response. I recalled the fullness of that time, all the life, warmth, and color in it. There was one moment in particular that I remember most.

My father, Rico, Antonio, and I stayed in a suite together at Caesars Palace, which was the venue of the fight. My cousins and I played in the hotel's arcade and ran around the complex feeling the pre-fight electricity in the air. My father treated Rico and Antonio like they were his sons, so we were all well-traveled and comfortable together. We were the only children to make that trip. My father was different in that way. He always wanted to share with us the good things he experienced.
180

I remember the sparkle in his eye moments before the great Leonard-Hagler fight. He told the three of us it was time to get ready. I was young but mature, having spent the majority of my time around older people. I emulated Rico and Antonio as best I could, so when I went into my father's part of the suite to get dressed there was a problem. My father had bought us boys new outfits for the fight. Rico and Antonio picked out white Benetton sweat suits and excitedly got dressed in their sporty outfits in the other part of the suite. I imagined the same type of outfit would be laid out for me on the bed, but my father had other plans.

I watched him with his shirt off, brushing his hair in the mirror in our side of the suite. I wasn't surprised to see his Versace laid out on the bed. I was surprised, however, to see a similar outfit laid out for me right next to his. The sharp creases in the little dress pants and the button-up shirt and vest were the complete opposite of how I wanted to dress for the fight. I wanted to dress young and sporty like my cousins. I emulated my dad the most. I tried to walk the way he walked, and I'd poke my bottom lip out the way his naturally poked out, but that night my cousins' influence was stronger. I had been one of the boys on the trip, and I wanted to keep things that way. So I just stood there, not moving toward the clothes that were clearly laid out for me. I was waiting for him to produce my Benetton sweat suit.

"What you waiting on, Slugg?" my father said as he turned to me. "You want me to dress you?" He continued flashing his bright, white smile.

"I don't want to wear that," I said, pointing at the outfit.

"Why?"

"I want to wear my sweat suit like Rico and 'Tonio."

"Nah, not tonight. Tonight you wearing that right there."

"But, Daddy..." I saw the seriousness of his face and knew that he meant it. I started crying.

"I don't know what you crying for, Slugg."

With tears in my eyes, I pleaded my case again, "'Cause I want to wear what Rico and 'Tonio are wearing."

He got the message that time, but instead of relenting as he often would, he said something to me that I couldn't understand then. "You ain't like everybody else. Understand? Look at me when I'm talking to you. You ain't like everybody else. Now come on and put these pants on."

He dressed me quickly in the outfit that I persisted to protest against. I wouldn't look at him even as he kneeled before me with my jewelry in his hand. He took my hand in his and slid my ring on my finger. The ring was gold with our initials T.L. encrusted in diamonds. He then wrapped the gold bracelet around my wrist, which was made up of my full name woven in cursive, and finally, as I reluctantly bent my head down a bit, he put the small gold chain around my neck. I watched him finish dressing himself in much the same fashion, and then we were off to the fight.

The detailing of our trip to Vegas in *Dream City* is factual but not accurate. The authors were not there, and they didn't care to put themselves there, wrestling on the page with the complexity of the human condition. Instead, they shaped a sensational story based on reports from law enforcement officers and fringe individuals with agendas. Back then, I wondered how much they really knew. Did they know while on that Vegas trip Alta Rae Zanville babysat for me, Rico, and Antonio? She was an acquaintance of Rayful's, a middle-aged white woman that he had randomly met. At first, he used her to put things in her name for him, and he eventually involved her in the drug business. She later would be one of the prosecution's star witnesses against Rayful. Obviously, I knew none of this as a child, just that she was a stranger given the responsibility to watch my cousins and me for a night. The three of us together were a handful. I was the most well mannered, then Rico, then Antonio. Still, given the degrees of our temperament, we all could be rambunctious, and we worked on her, trying to influence her to let us do what we wanted to do. It was late, well past the time we should have been out of the suite, but we wanted to go back to the arcade. Rightly, Ms. Zanville refused. No matter what we did, she just wouldn't let us out. After her final refusal, which was the most firm, Antonio struck the woman.

My father never left me with strangers, but it was an unusual trip. As the *Dream City* account details, my father and Rayful happened to meet Melvin Butler at that time. Butler was attracted to them. My dad already had his own lesser California connection and Rayful had his various drug connections. Yet in an instant Butler became the figure that forever linked my father and Rayful as partners.

As a student in Professor Helou's class, I wasn't quite ready to articulate my understanding of the war on drugs, and I certainly wasn't ready to talk about my family's involvement in it. So after class one day, I approached Professor Helou, revealing my identity and asking for his discretion in our discussion of that particular section of *Dream City*. Professor Helou handled the situation beautifully, which is another reason why I admire him so.

In 2003, I was placed at the Kennedy Recreation Center located in D.C.'s historic Shaw community. It was my first solo roving leader assignment. The rec was a new state-of-the-art facility, a total renovation of the place once known as Kennedy Playground. Aunt Bonnie used to take Kim, Alan, and me to Kennedy when we were little. The playground had towering sliding boards that frightened me. I've never been able to stand great heights, and as a child roller coasters also were out. I was a scared little guy; boats, swimming pools, clowns, the dark all frightened me, yet I never feared people. My cousin Kim feared nothing! While I watched in awe, she'd attack those sliding boards, making them her personal apparatus for adventure and experimentation. She'd slide down them face first, sideways, twisting and turning, and even backwards.

Anyway, the crew in that community took on the name of the playground. The guys from around 7th and O Street called themselves KDP. Growing up, my crew didn't mix much with KDP even though they were only six blocks away. This is often the case for kids in the inner city. You stay confined to your street.

With the Kennedy Rec Center being so close to Hanover, I was familiar with some of the guys from that community. We weren't friends, but we weren't enemies either, which was important given the work I was doing. Still, given my ties and various alliances from my not-too-distant past, I was cautious early on in my career.

It took a while, but eventually KDP accepted me as though I were one of their own. From the start, I was strategic and deliberate about my presence and work in the community. I understood the importance of quiet action at first. I had to prove myself worthy and trustworthy through work, not talk, and I couldn't be eager to connect. The community, and specifically the youth I worked with directly, was watching me closely. Their neighborhood was tough, and many of them, at the very least, were familiar with the adults in their lives disappointing them. It made them guarded. Not that they did not know love, but constant love, that consistency of kindness and love devoid of dysfunction, was the exception rather than the rule, and many of the children that I worked with didn't know how to receive it. They didn't know how to react to it or were suspicious of it. "What's this? Is he trying to take advantage of me in some way? Is this some kind of hustle?" I'll never forget the strange look I got from a child at KDP when I patted him on the head and told him that I was proud of him. He looked at me and didn't know how to respond. It was very likely that it was the first time a man, or perhaps even a woman for that matter, had ever uttered those words to him. It broke my heart. This is the kind of thing that's happening in the hood, and in my first assignment at KDP I worked hard to combat it. I took my groups on exposure field trips, did service projects with them, made home visits and school visits, coached basketball and flag football, and, when it came down to it, mediated disputes and squashed beefs.

The skills I had developed in interrupting violence during my 1st and O days served me well as a community worker. One of my first major reconciliations happened while I worked at the Kennedy Rec. Two young men, Vern and Gene, each sixteen years old at the time, were the best of friends. The two of them were inseparable, always right by each other's side during the various extracurricular programs I coordinated. Yet, when I arrived at work one day, I was informed that during a dispute Vern had shot Gene in the chest. I immediately reached out to both Vern and Gene and, with the help of another community outreach worker named Curtis Mozie, was able to arrange a sit-down meeting with them.

Vern tried to kill Gene. Mediating a situation like this is one of the toughest you'll ever have, but I had been there. I not only knew what their lives looked like but also what their lives *could* look like.

With the three of us sitting down in the rec, I told them how much I loved them and shared with them some of my experiences. I pled with them not to meet the fates I'd seen. They were engaged by my words, but I believe my effectiveness in convincing them to reconcile didn't just come in the words I spoke. First, the two of them truly did love and respect each other. That's big. I had to pull that out of them, help them to recognize that again. I also knew what tone to use, how close to get each of them, how to mine their ambivalence and lay bare their thought processes. After a heated exchange at the table, Gene was about to leave, and Vern was adamant about not letting him. I knew what he was thinking. If we were to let Gene leave, he'd be coming back to kill Vern. He'd be waiting for him. I brought all of this to light, and after much emotion and energy spent, those two young men hugged, reestablished their friendship, and never harmed one another again.

I learned another kind of reconciliation was possible while I was working at Kennedy Rec. Working as a roving leader in 2003, I coordinated a program called Business Explorers with Sarah Von Schrader from the Northwest Settlement House. We took teens from the Shaw community to observe professions and working professionals in fields that interested them. One of the youth said he wanted to be a police officer. I had become very friendly with a police captain named Diane Groomes (she's now the assistant chief of MPD). We had participated on the Ward 2 core team together and had put together a very successful program called "Curfew and Courts." I asked her if we could bring the group in to see her working, to which she gladly

187

said yes.

We arrived at the 3rd district precinct, and Captain Groomes gave our group a tour. At the time, walking through that place was strange. I wasn't that far removed from hanging on the block, and as we toured I recognized a lot of the officers that used to patrol our neighborhood. I didn't like them and they didn't like me, but some of them had seen me working in my role at Kennedy so we were cordial. As we continue to walk, Captain Groomes introduced us to vice Squad, where we ran into Officer Ortiz. After Captain Groomes unnecessarily introduced me and Ortiz, she started speaking glowingly about the positive impact I was making at Kennedy. Ortiz looked shocked, confused, and then ashamed. The vice squad presented their work to our group, and after their presentation, Ortiz asked if he could speak with me. Off to the side, he apologized to me with tears in his eyes. He said he just didn't know. I told him I forgave him and to think about me when he sees young men on the corner. Some of them are up to illegal behavior, but a lot more of them are there because they have nowhere else to go.

Reconciling with Officer Ortiz was a revelation for me. It happened very early in my career when I still was not sure of my purpose. But his coming to comprehension before me confirmed it. I had a mission. I would be an example of possibility for those who came up like me, and a bridge for the powerless and powerful to cross to gain a better understanding of each other's circumstance. And I'd continue living on Hanover as I did.

A Man for Others

I n May of 2004, I graduated Magna Cum Laude from UDC. The accomplishment was as significant if not more significant than my graduation from Gonzaga. At the age of twenty-four, I had transformed my life. I was determined to dedicate all my effort to the work of serving the less fortunate with compassion, wit, and an ever-evolving perspective on the challenges therein.

My family and friends helped me celebrate the achievement on graduation day. Aunt Bonnie wrote to my father in prison to describe the time to him. Her words reflect the moment best.

Tony:

Just a few lines to share our experience with Tony's graduation. It was a glorious day. He was so very happy; what an accomplishment...Alvin and I gave him a cookout for his graduation. It was spectacular; it reminded you of the old Hanover of years gone by. There was a hell of a turnout for your son... I cooked and fed a many people that day; we had something for them. Our menu included outside deep fried fish, fried chicken, ribs, grilled chicken, hot dogs, hamburger, baked beans, pota-

to salad, macaroni and shrimp salad, deviled eggs, and so many bottles of champagne that lots of his guests brought. It lasted until 10:30 that night. The weather was exceptional that day; it was as if God himself was not going to allow nothing to rain on his parade. There were no fights or arguments; it was truly beautiful...

How are things with you? Hopefully good. There were some very distinguished guests at the graduation, including former mayor Marion Barry, renowned brain surgeon Dr. Ben Carson, Congressman Charles Rangel, and a number of others. Check out the program I have included on the ceremony. Tony's name is on page 17; I have highlighted his name...

The highs in my life feel so heavenly because the lows have been so devastating. A short time before my graduation, in nearly the same spot that Lil' Dennis died, my good friend Jon Jon was shot and killed. Being Cornell Jones's nephew, Jon Jon was more like family. I had known him my entire life. His death moved me to tears like I had never been moved before. For years, after seeing so much death, I was left unable to cry. But at Jon Jon's funeral my tear ducts opened up and I cried hard. I cried for Jon Jon and the many friends, like my man June, that I could not find tears for at the time of their passing. I cried and cried, and when my tears dried, I vowed that I would do every-thing in my power, beyond my power, to positively impact the communities in Washington D.C. where untimely death, violence, incarceration, and hopelessness were too much an everyday reality.

I needed all the surety and confidence I could muster in my move from working with youth to ex-offenders. My entrance into this next phase of my career was working for Project Empowerment. Project Empowerment (PE) provides supportive services, adult basic education, job coaching, employability, life skills and limited vocational training, and job search assistance to District of Columbia residents living in areas with high unemployment and/or poverty levels. PE's mission is to reduce widespread joblessness among the District's hard-to-serve population with multiple employment barriers (e.g., ex-offenders) and successfully move them into the workforce.

I was hired in 2005, right after Hurricane Katrina. In the aftermath of the storm, a large displaced group from New Orleans was given refuge at the D.C. Armory. As an outreach worker, I was among the people there to support the victims. Seeing them come off the plane, heads bowed, still wearing dirty and water-beaten clothes, affected me deeply. Many of them didn't even know where they were, having been told they'd be flown to Dulles airport and mistakenly hearing Dulles as Dallas. I saw their pain and felt it as if it were my own, which drove me to do all I could to help them. Every day for a month, I worked inexhaustibly hard at the Armory's recreation center, providing fresh clothes, support, and personal care. Working with them, looking into their eyes, hearing their stories, sharing bits about each other's cultures, and laughing with them reaffirmed for me the power of compassionate service.

Many don't think of ex-offenders as a population in great need because of the stigma attached to criminals in this country. There's also the invisibility, which may be even more powerful than the scarlet letter branded on criminals here. You hear about the crimes they commit, the arrest, the charge, and the sentencing, but then they vanish into the prison system and are forgotten. Our current prison system is highly effective at forever disappearing folk who commit crimes. They are gone when inside and gone when they come out, forgotten and not seen by all but the communities they come home to, that is if they are able to come home. I've been working with ex-offenders for eight years and having worked with disadvantaged groups of all kinds during that time, I can say with confidence that the children of ex-offenders and ex-offenders themselves are two of the most disadvantaged groups in the country, who also happen to receive the least amount of support.

Professionally, I began supporting ex-offenders as a job coach, or officially manpower development specialist, at PE. I'd go visit my clients on their worksites and mediate any disputes or issues they had at work. I'd also provide them with continuous professional development and advocate on their behalf to get hired permanently. After a year and a half of working in that role, I was asked to become a facilitator. A facilitator at PE is like a teacher and coach who leads a classroom full of newly released ex-offenders. Even before I committed to the position full time, I had already had some experience with it, as I'd be used as a substitute whenever one of the full-time facilitators would take off work. The change from job coach to facilitator was a promotion that I did not apply for or request. But our director at PE, Charles Jones, must have seen something in me.

In the span of three weeks, a facilitator has to best prepare newly released ex-offenders for their new lives in the world, particularly in their efforts to join the workforce. The course was a combination of life skills and job training. Initially, we used a curriculum by Gordon Graham called "Breaking Barriers," which was a series really created for those who were still incarcerated. After a year or so using that curriculum and augmenting it with my own scholarship, perspective, and insight, I was asked to create a curriculum that would be a revision of Graham's work. So I did. I also convinced our director to get smart boards for each classroom so that the lessons could be more modern and interactive. The returning citizens were not coming back to a world of chalk and blackboards. We were in the digital age, and they had to be prepared for that.

Coincidentally, Shakey and Alan were in the first class I facilitated at Project Empowerment. Before I started working at PE, I, along with other roving leaders, was asked to recommend individuals for the program that PE offered. They didn't have to be recently released from prison—they just had to have a charge and come from certain hotspots in the city. Hanover was still a hot spot, so I recommended Alan and Shakey because I really thought the program would be helpful. I had no idea at the time that shortly thereafter, I would be hired at Project Empowerment, and I certainly couldn't have seen me moving to the role of facilitator as quickly as I did. But these kinds of ironies have occurred frequently in my life.

Shakey had always been in the streets with me, but Alan was just starting to really get out there. The door to that life was opened wider when his father got sick.

Uncle Boo fell ill in the mid-nineties with neurosarcoidosis, a painful disease in which the nervous system becomes inflamed, and in 1999 Alan came to live with us on Hanover permanently. After my father went to prison, Uncle Boo was the man I most tried to be like. Boo was widely respected. He could go any-where in the city, the toughest hoods, and wouldn't have any trouble. In many ways, Boo was there for me the same way he was for my father when he was a boy. Boo understood the humanity of the people that came through the same conditions he did. A lesson I learned from him as a boy is an example of this.

By the age of twelve, I had seen a lot and thought I knew it all. One day, I was out with Uncle Boo on 7th and T Street, and we were approached by a drug addict. I watched Uncle Boo give some money to the man and said, "Boo, why you gon give money to that pipe head?"

He turned to me. "Slugg, let me tell you a little something about life. Them pipe heads you're talking about are people. Some of 'em are my friends, and I knew 'em before they got like that. They just sick. Sometimes you got to take care of your

194

people like that. You'll see what I'm saying when you get my age."

I never forgot that lesson, and I think about it from time to time when I'm caring for others.

With Uncle Boo's illness, there have been many times that I've had to care for him. He now lives with his daughter, Kim. Boo still has a passion for gambling, but now because of his health, Kim tries to restrict him from going to the crap joint as freely. He needs us to take him there and quite often needs money from us to gamble with. He's crafty in the ways he tries to work on us, coolly evoking the past sometimes, which I coolly dismiss. Back then we were children and he was gambling to take care of us. Now that we're adults, we don't need that, but he still needs to gamble.

My relationship with Alan was very much like the relationship I had in my younger years with Rico and Antonio. Being three years older than Alan, I always schooled him on the things I knew. When Uncle Boo got sick, I had already been through a similar situation with my parents, and I'd talk to him about it, making sure I was for him what I once wished I had. Beyond the hardship of his transition, it was fun having him around all the time. Though I had plenty of friends, having a little brother in the house was a welcomed addition.

But when Alan started hitting the streets hard, I got concerned. It was tough for him because he really started getting out at the time I was transitioning off the block. And there had always been subtle comparisons in the family. I had always gotten good grades, but Alan wasn't the best student, and certain members of the family would say things like, "See, Tony. You should be more like him."

But Alan was being like me, the street side of me, and I alone understood fully what he was going through. Alan wasn't a criminal; he dabbled in selling drugs a little bit and hung on the block, but he wasn't a street dude. Before he moved to Hanover, he and Kim would always be around there, but they grew up in Maryland and they lived a comfortable suburban life all the way up until the time Uncle Boo got sick.

But if you're going to be out there, you're going to get into trouble, you're going to be exposed. And by being my cousin, Alan was ushered into it. My old crew immediately took him in, and Alan and Shakey really got tight. I would talk to Alan all the time—not preaching, I never preach—and I tried to share the alternatives with him. That's what the Project Empowerment recommendation was about. I was willing to try anything.

For the next few years, I taught ex-offender classes every day from 9 a.m. to 4 p.m. As in all things one hopes to develop mastery in, I had to hone my craft over time as a teacher. But I did well at the job from the start, and progress from my starting point happened quickly. Everything in my life up until that point had been the greatest preparation and training for that role. Since I started teaching ex-offenders at twenty-five, my age was my biggest challenge. The average age of participants in the program was thirty-seven. Quite a few of the participants were twice my age and had children older than me. I know they were wondering what I had to say to them, what I knew. "Look at him, a baby, they got this baby in here. What is he going to teach me about living?"

It wasn't that I didn't have much still to learn myself. I had a lot of life ahead of me and much learning and many new experiences to look forward to. I never approached my instruction from an authoritarian perspective. I was the leader and the facilitator, but I viewed my classes as a shared experience. I went in knowing that I would learn some things from the participants as well. But I quickly gained their respect in that, for the most part, I knew all about the life they had lived on the street. However, I was living a life that most, if not all of them, knew nothing about. Yet, with all of me, I wanted them to know about that life. I wanted them to be able to be there for those they left at home—their children. I taught with these goals in mind.

It was going to be incredibly hard, especially given all the blockades the law and society has put in place for ex-offenders. Unfortunately, the phrase "paid their debt to society" is a relic of the past. Today, ex-offenders keep paying, dearly, when they re-enter society. It's unjust.

Still, despite the injustice, you can make it. You can make it living on the straight and narrow with unwavering faith, patience that's often painful, and work that begins very humbly. You can completely transform your life and live in a newness that feels like a dream.

I facilitated with this dream on my mind and in my heart,

knowing it was mostly up to the participant and God to get it right, but hoping and praying that something I might say or do in that class or even outside of it—because I was always available for them—could help. I knew I was starting to make an impact when strangers started coming up to me on the street and telling me that their friend or cousin, uncle or aunt had taken my class and spoke very highly of me. Now, these are street people from a culture that's known for not giving others their due, especially not in the field I was working in. But I'd be out and about and people would come up to me and not only tell me about the class, but also about jobs. Telling me I got so and so a job, thanking me, and often asking me if I could look into getting them a job as well. The word spread not only through the city, but also in the prison system, and participants literally started requesting me as their facilitator. These moments make all the hard work and occasional disappointments worth it. For me, few things make me feel better than helping a person get on the right track and watching them stay on it. Years later, I've run into former clients who are still employed and approaching that dream. Meeting up with them in those moments is a tremendous feeling. Yet the numbers are few, and there's still so much work to do.

One of the reasons we haven't made more progress in supporting ex-offenders is because their predicament hasn't gotten the exposure it needs. In 2007, I was approached by a producer from the cable network BET about their *American Gangster* documentary series. The network was in the process of making an episode on Rayful and contacted me to get to my father. They wanted my dad to be a participant, but he flatly refused. The producer was discouraged, but I saw the connection as an opportunity to cast a positive light on our ex-offender program. Given that many of the ex-offender participants at Project Empowerment were imprisoned as a result of the drug trade during the crack era, I invited the producer to one of my classes. My father had practically ordered me to stay away from the project, and I didn't really have a desire or the expectation that I'd be in it. Truthfully, I just wanted someone from the outside world to see the work we were doing, and perhaps they might go back and spread the word. But when the producer saw me teach and heard the type of things I talked about—I didn't put on any special show—she became interested in me being a part of the documentary. When I expressed some hesitation, the producer told me they'd only ask me questions about D.C. during that time, and as a bonus they'd get some footage of me in the classroom as well. That sold me. I ran it all by my father, trying to convince him of the positive impact it could have, and after he considered all that I had presented, he gave me his blessing.

BET later did an *American Gangster* episode on Cornell Jones, which I was also a part of. I'm less vocal in Cornell's episode. Wearing a "Free Tony Lewis" t-shirt, I silently stroll down Hanover with Cornell and listen to him reminisce of days gone by. Being on television was exciting, and it certainly raised my profile throughout the city. I'd been working in relative obscurity for years, but suddenly a bright light had been cast on me. I was most happy about the national exposure our work with ex-offenders had received—the more the better.

It's 2008, and it's 2 a.m. I'm over at a lady friend's house, and we're asleep in bed together. My phone rings. I ignore it. It rings a second time and I miss the call, but I look to see who the call was coming from. It's from a guy named Ahmad who lives around 1st and O. As I'm about to dial, the phone rings again. I pick up. There's yelling on the other end. *What? What? No. Aw, man. Don't tell me that. Don't tell me that. Please don't tell me that. Please tell me you're joking—not Alan.*

I jump up and throw my clothes on. I'm talking to myself the entire time. *Come on, man. Not, Alan. Come on, Alan. Come on.* I throw the bedroom door open, fly down the stairs, and get into my car. I pound the steering wheel over and over and I scream. Then I start the car and speed to the scene, running every red light and every stop sign along the way.

I had just been with Alan earlier that day. He was still living with me and Grandma, but we didn't hang out as much any-more since I had so many more competing outside demands on my life. Plus, he and I spent a lot of nights with our girlfriends. But we had just been together that entire day. We went to get my car out of the shop, worked out together, went to the store to buy me a new cell phone, and finally picked his girlfriend up from work.

I'm driving thinking it just can't be. *Not, Alan. Please.* I get around 1st and O and see a bunch of people, an ambulance, and some police cars. I park my car, walk over, and make my way through the crowd. Then I see Alan lying on the pavement.

He was dead.

Shakey saw it happen. He and Alan were hanging out with the rest of the crew. Shake was sitting in the car, and Alan was sitting on the hood. They were talking to each other when some guys came through shooting. Alan wasn't the target. He wasn't involved at all, but he was hanging with the crew. No one else got hit. But Alan was struck by a bullet in the head.

I used to tell Alan, "Please do something different, if not for your sake then for mine." Now he was gone, and the reaction I feared was bubbling up uncontrollably inside me. I wanted vengeance. Fuck peace.

Many Thousands Gone

I grew up with killers who didn't need a contract to avenge Alan's murder. All I had to do was give the word and, to be honest, I considered it. But I couldn't do it. At my weakest, I thought how could I claim to be a servant of the people and be contemplating murderous revenge? Wasn't I a God-fearing man? Wasn't this the very spirit and mentality I was working to eradicate? Looking into the eyes of the people I worked with daily reminded me of this. But not long after Alan's death, I still wore the appearance of revenge.

At the funeral, an elder from around our way saw the look in my eyes and approached me. Staring directly at me, he opened his mouth and simply said, "Nah." Then he hugged me tightly. One word and a strong, loving embrace—he knew I had to move forward, and I knew I had to move forward. I had to be strong, again, and continue to forge ahead in peace. But first, I had to release my burden. I needed to talk to God. I had to talk to him. And, later, I had to talk to a therapist.

I went to see a therapist once a week for a couple of months, and through the course of my therapy I realized by not allowing violent retribution for Alan's murder, I had passed the greatest test of my life. The initial feelings of rage, sadness, and disappointment were natural emotions, but I grew up in an unnatural environment. I saw and experienced things that made me think, feel, and react abnormally. Every day I guard against this proclivity. Yet I've also learned to fully embrace who I am. As I progressed, I didn't run away from my past. Instead, I wrestled with it and worked to make sense of it. I found light in the darkest places, and now I use it to help others find their way through.

Together, prayer and therapy can heal, but there's not nearly enough of either happening in the hood, and they especially aren't being done together. Given all the suffering, stacked up through all the years, downtrodden communities of color need a revival of mind and spirit. There must be a paradigm shift, a movement that supports counselors, upstanding clergy, psychiatrists, psychologists, and authentic champions of peace and justice in these impoverished places. Step by step and with collective action, it can happen. I very much need it to happen. Because looking in Shakey's eyes and seeing the pain and knowing he's not being helped tears me to pieces. Shakey's seen what I've seen. All those traumatic things can't be dealt with alone. But he won't seek help.

It's cultural. We have to work to change that culture. There are so many others that need help, and it pains me to no end knowing the weight they carry daily. We have to help them. We have to help them help themselves. We have to unburden them. For if not, eventually, they will become burdens to us all.

After Alan's death, I didn't immediately seek therapy. I worked through it like I always had until another event a few months later triggered my urgency to seek help.

I was manning a detail at D.C. Jail through Project Empowerment. I was selected to lead the new employment readiness center there. The placement called for me to go inside the prison for the first time. Quantico was different. It was a military base that had a small place for prisoners, and it wasn't a prison in and of itself. But inside D.C. Jail I was actually on the cellblock. I had never experienced prison in that way. "So this is what my loved ones see," I thought. I didn't experience the dread other visitors have said they feel when those prison doors closed behind you, locking you in. I felt fine. I felt more than fine. The sound of the doors, the popping of the cells, the correctional officers, all of it felt familiar.

While there, I fell into a manner I didn't know I had. During lunch breaks, I did pull-ups on the back of the iron prison stairs with the inmates. Once, a correctional officer was looking for me in the TV room but couldn't pick me out of a crowd of inmates because I had so immersed myself. Though I didn't have on an orange jump suit, I had to raise my hand and say, "I'm right here," for her to spot me.

Later, one of the inmates said to me, "Mr. Lewis, you're way too comfortable in this joint to have never been up in one of these joints."

It jarred me. I kept my composure until I got off work, but when I got off the clock, I let go and had a full-blown crisis of conscience. How and why am I so comfortable in prison?

Through the course of the therapy, I learned that I expected to be there. Grandma had a similar feeling much earlier in my life. There must have been a point in my life that I accepted my own incarceration as inevitable. Going to prison became the natural order of things in my neighborhood. It wasn't just my family, but most of my friends too. Growing up, we began to view prison like young people from affluent communities viewed going to college.

The United States has the highest incarceration rate in the world. We also have the most incarcerated people in the world. To put this in perspective, the total number of prisoners in the United States is greater than the total number of prisoners in China, a country that has 1.3 billion people, which is nearly five times the population of our country. Silently, mass incarceration has become a major problem in the United States.

The explosive growth of our prison population in the last twenty plus years is directly connected to the war on drugs. In the mid 1980s, Congress passed sweeping legislation, including the prejudiced mandatory minimum drug laws, in order to give the ongoing drug war full support. To date, the policies and procedures have been largely ineffective in stopping the sale and use of illicit drugs in this country. Yet, it has been quite effective in targeting and imprisoning poor black and brown men, assuring our country maintains the ignoble distinction of being the world's greatest jailer. The continuous work and incredible sacrifices made by citizens of all colors, cultures, and creeds has made the United States today a freer country than it has ever been. However, intolerance, masked discriminatory public policy, and its enforcement continues to mar our great country.

The genius of the war on drugs is the program's ability to justify discrimination. It's harder to point out the injustice when those most affected *have* committed drug crimes. The selling and use of illegal drugs is not the exclusive territory of poor black and brown people. Yet, when one looks at those sentenced for non-violent drug crimes it appears that way. A clear double standard exists. Those not from impoverished communities use and sell drugs nearly free from worry. They understand that their privilege gives them relative immunity from the law.

In the crack era, black drug dealers were mythologized and sensationalized right along with crack cocaine. Those who were old enough during the mid-eighties and early nineties will remember a number of nationally run commercials that vilified black drug dealers and sensationalized the impact of illegal narcotics. This media push worked on the psyche of the masses in such a way that few questioned the fairness of newly drafted mandatory minimum drug laws. During this time, the phrase "drug dealer" became etched in the minds of the masses as synonymous with black men. Drug dealers were all black men and bad men. This characterization, coupled with the country's long-held suspect view of black men, helped the new drug legislations and subsequent enforcement gain support from the masses, if not directly than indirectly. The violence associated with crack also helped toward this end. But lawmakers and those in positions of power took the wrong approach to this danger. Excessive spending on law enforcement and draconian drug laws enforced primarily against the poor was not the answer.

Especially in the absence of jobs, poorly educated people are more likely to become violent. Law enforcement is needed, but to cause a drastic reduction in violent crimes and change the culture of violence in poor communities, far more emphasis should be placed on properly educating the children of those communities and creating jobs for their parents. But this wasn't done in the 1980s when unemployment rates for the poor skyrocketed as a result of America's changing economy. The way we did business as a country changed, and the poor were left behind. They were left in jobless communities and in public schools that prepared them for jobs of a bygone American era. Jobless, undereducated, and discriminated against—isolated and made to be outcasts—underserved communities became centers of desperate survival, and with that came violence. Looking not to help these communities but to further their own agendas, fear mongers ran rampant with this condition. Along with the war on drugs, their determined efforts—fueled by sensational media coverage—worked to effectively criminalize poverty in black and brown communities. While awful things were happening in the hood, equally shameful things were happening in association on the Hill. People like me and my friends were most negatively affected.

I didn't find out that my father was sentenced to life without the possibility of parole until I was sixteen years old. I had been curious for years, and so one day while in the library at Gonzaga, I decided to do an Internet search about my father's case. I was led to believe he'd be coming home one day, but when I finally found out the truth, I wasn't shocked. Everyone had always been so optimistic, but something about the situation never felt right to me. When I talked to my father, his reassurances didn't have the same spark of hope in it as everyone else's. I recognize now that's because he knew the truth. Yet he had not told anyone in our family the truth, the actual terms of his sentence. I have a letter from Aunt Bonnie to my father where she says in one of the lines, "At least there's light at the end of the tunnel."

But there was no light. Not the kind of light Aunt Bonnie meant. Yet when she wrote those words, she sincerely thought my father could look forward to leaving prison. It was a common misunderstanding. At the time, anyone familiar with drug crimes thought receiving a life sentence meant twenty-five years to life, or a life sentence *with* the possibility of parole. Those were the type of sentences non-violent offending drug dealers used to receive.

Cornell Jones was one of the biggest drug dealers the country has ever seen. Before his major drug conviction, he had been in and out of prison as a young person, but the American justice system was very different when he came along. Back then, prison was viewed as a place of punishment and rehabilitation. Cornell is a product of this system. After he was caught for the operation on Hanover, he pled guilty and served nine years in prison. He's home now. Effectively rehabilitated, he never returned to prison after that last sentence. Fortunately, he went in before the enactment of the new drug laws. He had the opportunity to change his mentality. He was allowed to grow beyond his circumstances.

My father wasn't so fortunate. With mandatory minimums quietly put in place, the prosecution offered him a deal of thirty years for a guilty plea. 30 Thirty years? He knew about Cornell's plea deal and the deals other drug dealers had gotten before him. In comparison, the prosecutors' offer seemed like a joke. Thirty years? They had to be joking. No matter the amount of weight sold, drug dealers weren't offered plea deals for thirty years. That was for murderers. And for his first charge? No. He'd take his chances in court.

But he was up against the federal government, and this was 1989, when few outside of those working for the Department of Justice truly knew the in-depth details of the new drug laws. It was better that way, better to catch the "bad guys" by surprise and make examples out of them. Yet this wasn't a one-time example. This wasn't a judge coming down hard on my father in an effort to discourage such business in the future. No, the new drug laws stripped nearly all power of judgment away from judges, making them more like automatons devoid of resourceful thought, feeling, and perception. Once a model for the world, the new laws made a mockery of our legal system, and a number of longstanding judges stepped down in protest. *You mean every one? Despite his individual circumstance, criminal history, background, age, and appearance of contrition, you mean every one? Each is to be made an example?* Yes. *And for how long?*

Forever.

This system will continue on like this indefinitely unless people who know better, people of high principle and conscious, come together to force the dismantling of it. Poor black and brown men, many drug criminals by act and circumstance and not by character, will continue to be judged excessively and inhumanely by these laws, and there are residual effects. Even now, the system is affecting others. Injustice, eventually, tends to infiltrate unintended places. My mistreatment, if not corrected, likely will become yours. History has shown us this.

I believe my father deserves a second chance at life. His charges were his first convictions, which came at the age of twenty-six, and the nature of his crime was a non-violent drug offense. He deserves another chance, and nothing can convince me otherwise. In fact, I feel more strongly about this by the day.

My father didn't have the chance to grow to understand his energy and divine power. He never had someone who cared about him enough, some wise and powerfully spirited person whom he respected to be an example for him, to point out his light, to ponder the daily struggles of life with him, and to dream and work with him in seeking alternative possibilities. Yes, my father did what he did as a man of free will. No one made him sell the amount of drugs he sold. But agency isn't the only issue here. The drug laws of this country make my father's sentence, and many others who have sentences like his, more tragic than it should be.

After working at Project Empowerment for a few years, I moved on to the Court Services and Offender Supervision Agency (CSOSA). CSOSA is an independent federal agency that supervises D.C. residents on parole, probation, or supervised release. I train these individuals to get them ready for potential job opportunities. I also build relationships with employers and other agencies that will allow our clients opportunities for training, education, and employment.

Recently, I was part of a meeting with the mayor's office and CSOSA concerning St. Elizabeth—the mental institution to which my mother had been committed. In recent years, the bastion of mental health has fallen into disrepair, and as a result, the number of patients it treats and houses fell significantly. St. Elizabeth is divided into two campuses: the east campus, owned by the city, and the west campus, which is owned by the federal government. Each campus planned to begin large-scale renovations, and we were meeting with the mayor's office to discuss the best way to create a pipeline for our clients so that they might obtain gainful employment in every aspect of the project. We had not had any success on the west campus renovation, mainly because it was a federal project and the headquarters of Homeland Security, so our demographic was in direct opposition from a background standpoint. However, the east campus was a D.C. project, and we looked to have more luck with getting our clients engaged. While I sat in the meeting advocating and negotiating for my clients, powerful emotions churned inside of me. I couldn't help but think about all the times I visited my mother at St. E. All that she and I had gone through, and here I was at the negotiating table trying to help people find jobs to repair the place. Sitting at that meeting table, I looked for a glimpse of something in the eyes of the other men in the room. Had any of them had any personal experience with St. Elizabeth's? Did any of them understand the way I was feeling? I searched their eyes for that something that would tell me, but I didn't see anything. You don't get to that table—or any table like it—having seen what I've seen.

My mother's story continues. Today she lives alone in her own apartment supported by government aid. She's able to live independently as she's never been suicidal. Still, she's chronically mentally ill because she's not on any medication and hasn't been for years. She refuses to take it. As I mentioned before, the medicine that's available isn't a miracle drug. When taking it, she doesn't return to her old self, just a dimmed version of her new self, though it is somewhat helpful. I do know the SSI she receives normally doesn't last her past the tenth of the month because she never learned how to manage money properly. My mother calls me, Grandma, and friends for money to get her through the rest of the month, and this helps to put things in perspective. A lot of her money goes to casinos and playing the numbers. She has a gambling habit like most of my family. She gambles a lot with her friends when they can tolerate her, and if she can't find anyone to go with her, she goes alone.

However, most of her days are spent walking her community, which is only about twelve blocks around Hanover. Sometimes she'll stand in the lobby of her apartment building and argue with people who aren't there, which prompts security. She'll then call me and tell me to come get her because they're trying to kill her. She calls me often throughout the day, some days dozens and dozens of times. She'll say things like people are shooting through the floor of her apartment, or they're trying to turn her into a prostitute, or they say that they're going to kill her because she snitched on my father. Most times, I don't answer, or when I do answer, sometimes we start arguing because I forget that she's sick. I just so badly want her to realize all the things she says are completely irrational. Those things she worries about do happen, and she's seen them happen, but they are not happening to her. I'm only human and it's my mother, so I get swept up in the moment and I forget these delusions are part of her condition.

She calls me a lot for money when she wants to go gamble, but I'm learning not to enable her. Many times I've tried to take her out and hang out, but there is nothing normal about it. There's always someone after us or someone trying to kill us. She will randomly turn to people and say, "I see you, mother-fucker. You ain't gonna do shit to us."

I'll be driving and she'll say, "Tony hurry up! Turn this way not that way!" I worry so much about her. I dread the day some stranger doesn't understand her illness and hurts her. Often I receive calls from friends who say, "I saw your mother walking on N Street, talking to herself." Most of the people close to me know about my mother's affliction. I'm not at all embarrassed by it. That's the way it is.

My mother has an advocate (power of attorney) appointed by the court, but he wants to give her case up because she is so unmanageable. He was appointed her guardian in 1999 but doesn't check up on her often because she stopped going to her outpatient services and getting her meds long ago. Our mental health system in this country needs reevaluation. The deinstitutionalization movement hasn't worked well for people like my mother. I don't know if she should be committed full time, but I do know she's a danger to herself in public, though she doesn't fight strangers; in her illness she's never touched a person she doesn't know. She does, however, say some alarming things to people, and there's always the potential for physical conflict when that happens because someone just might not understand. But most of the time my mother stays in her community where everyone knows her, and so that gives me some peace.

None of the friends my mother had before she became ill spend time with her except for Peanut, who is Tracie's aunt. She has a couple of girlfriends that she gambles with, but I hardly know them, and they seem to only hang with her when she has some money. I do my best for my mother, but no matter what I do or no matter what I give, it's never enough. The times I don't give in at all to her requests she'll say, "You don't do shit for me." Though I know her words are untrue, they still hurt, deeply.

My family has always called my mother Mona, a nickname for Samone. I keep my mother of old framed in my mind. She's encased in impenetrable glass and heavily guarded. She's a masterpiece, my Mona Lisa, and I turn inward often to gaze at her for perspective. I am growing and learning to fully appreciate all that she means to me today.

In 2003, my father was moved from the maximum-security prison in Lompoc, California, to a medium-security prison in Cumberland, Maryland. I was ecstatic. Now I have the opportunity to see him far more frequently. Cumberland is only a two and a half hour drive from D.C. I'm so very thankful that, today, whenever my schedule is free, I can drive to see him. A visiting room isn't home, but it's the closest thing to it. On our visits, we talk a lot about the past, catching up for all those years we weren't able to see each other. We talk about the present and the future too, and the everyday things that are best communicated face to face. Though I've always spoken to him regularly on the telephone and wrote letters and emails, there's no substitute for visits. They're essential. They help to keep our connection strong while also keeping him physically connected to the outside world.

The other day I went to visit my father, and one of the correctional officers struck up a conversation with me on the way out. The guards are friendlier with me now that I've received a fair bit of press locally. I remained there only a couple of hours, and the officer pointed out the shortness of the visit. I smiled at her and said, "Well, after twenty-four years, you learn to be more efficient. You can get in and out."

The officer looked at me in amazement. "Twenty-four years?"

She couldn't believe it and commended me for the longevity. She said she had been an officer for fifteen years and had become accustomed to seeing the attrition. "Many don't make it two years," she said. The officer was specifically talking about visits, but keeping a consistent connection in general is hard.

Millions know the pain of being on the other side, trying to hold onto your family or a dear friend who's imprisoned. You get better at some things, finding efficient routines that work, but the fatigue of it is something that you never get used to. The task can be emotionally exhausting, especially as the years add up. Visiting prisons as long as I have does something to you. It's been especially difficult for me over the years because of the amount of people I know who are incarcerated and how vigilant

I've been with them all through the years. At times, it can be overwhelming. When you're intimately connected with some-one who's incarcerated, it's as if you're doing the time with him. Every day I press the number five on my telephone. It is the number you must select to accept a phone call from an inmate who's in federal prison. It's usually my father, but if it's not him or my cousins Rico and Antonio, then it's someone from the neighborhood that I know. The word has spread over the years. Guys start talking, and my number gets passed along. Naturally, when they call I pick up. I'm one to always pick up. I've long been this kind of conduit.

Inmates cannot send mail directly to each other, but they can send mail to an intermediary on the outside who can then re-direct the letter or package to the other inmate. Since my early teens, I've served as that kind of mail courier not only for my father, but for many others who were incarcerated. I was the responsible one, the one who cared consistently. *Send it to Slugg, and he'll make sure you'll get it.* 39 Hanover Place was like the United States Post Office, UPS, and FedEx all in one for my incarcerated loved ones. For years, I did it gladly. It was the least I could do. I was free, and I understood more than most what they were going through. But over time my help in this capacity was taken for granted. It became thankless work, and as my life's responsibilities continued to increase, the mail didn't stop.

One day, I lost a letter my father had written to a friend. I don't know how I lost it. I had a good system, but the letter was

218

gone. I spoke to my father over the telephone and told him what had happened. He scolded me. At that point, I was twenty-nine years old and had been providing this particular courier service for many years, in addition to all other forms of personal communication with imprisoned friends and family members. And, on top of all that I had going on in my life, it became too much. A few days later, I was sitting in my bedroom with a lap full of letters that needed to be mailed off, and I just broke down. Hearing my father's voice scolding me, I took a letter he had prepared for someone else and tore it up in a fit.

Being that consistent connection creates the kind of expectation that at times is difficult to live up to. As the years go by, it wears away at you. This is why so many people, friends and family members, fall out of communication with prisoners over time. The burden of the attachment becomes too great. Often, inmates don't understand the trials their family and friends face on the outside and how that impacts their ability to keep up communication. Or the work and sacrifice it takes to keep that connection strong.

Money is often a point of tension. Inmates can work, but often family and friends will put money in their commissary, which is a kind of prison bank account. In prison, communication costs money. The least expensive form of communication for inmates is letters. Pen, paper, envelopes, and postage together are far less than the cost of phone calls. But hearing that familiar voice is important, and for poor families that cost can quickly add up. A type of email system called Corrlinks is the most recent form of communication put in place, but it too costs money and can get expensive because the inmates pay by the character.

Visits are the greatest way to keep the connection strong. When you're in that visiting hall together, the walls disappear and you just focus on being in your loved one's presence. Visits are the closest the incarcerated come to the outside world and being free in it.

Over the years, I've seen what has become of Appalachia on my visits to prisons. It began with our road trips to visit Uncle Greg at Lewisburg, PA, and continues today with my trips to see my father, cousins, and friends. On behalf of CSOSA, I also speak at federal prisons up and down the east coast. So there, in the brick and mortar, I've witnessed mass incarceration become a well-fortified institution in this country. In addition to the prison-industrial complex, where inmates get paid a pittance to manufacture goods for the public, prisons have also become the lifeblood of small towns across the U.S. The transformation of old economies, what used to be primarily steel and coal country, has become prison country. In Western Pennsylvania, there are Allenwood, Canaan, Lewisburg, Loretto, McKean, Moshannon Valley, and Schuykill. In West Virginia, there are Alderson, Beckley, Gilmer, Hazelton, Mcdowell, and Morgantown. That's thirteen federal prisons set up in hard-hit economic areas providing thousands of jobs. This is a small sampling of federal prisons in the two states I'm most familiar with. There are hundreds more: federal, state, and private prisons spread in remote areas across the country.

Driving through those remote areas on my way to a visit, I find myself thinking less about the big picture and more about the moment. Those drives demand that you remain focused on what's in front of you. FCI Cumberland, which is my father's prison, is in the mountains. I've driven to see him when the fog was so thick the prison wouldn't admit visitors because of the poor visibility. So I'd have to just turn right back around. Of course I have no choice but to keep my composure because the road ahead was incredibly foggy and I was driving down windy, mountainous roads alongside big rigs. Another time I was turned away because I was wearing a sweat suit. The dress code is serious while visiting a prison. There's a long list of things one must remember before setting out on a journey to a prison. For example, women can't wear underwire bras. It takes thought and preparation.

When Uncle Greg went back to prison in 2001, he was sent to USP Allenwood. Once when a few of us were going to visit him there, Grandma got turned away because she had undergone two knee replacements and the metal in her body kept setting off the metal detector. She had forgotten her medical card, which explained her condition, and had to miss the visit. Having fully patted her down and searched her, they still couldn't take the chance of letting her through. We understood, but after a four-hour drive for an old woman wanting to see her son, it was a big letdown. There was another time when going

221

to see Uncle Greg we stopped to get something to eat before arriving. Uncle Alvin had taken some of his high blood pressure medication with his food and didn't think anything about it. Well, when you go into these prisons they're not only checking for weapons but also drugs and other contraband. To test for drugs, they run a cloth over your pockets and your hands, and then run that through a machine. Doc didn't have any drugs on him, but the residue on his hands from his high blood pressure medication was enough to turn him away. My family was aging, and we were still making the trip. Knee replacements and high blood pressure pill residue were things we didn't have to think about before. Now we do.

My cousin Rico and my uncle Lo, who is Uncle Boo's wife's brother, were also incarcerated at Allenwood with Uncle Greg. Coincidentally, my barber and good friend, also named Rico, had an uncle incarcerated at Allenwood as well. Rico's uncle, Darrin, was serving a life sentence there for his role in the R Street crew drug conspiracy. Rico is nine years older than me and is from northeast Washington D.C. Before he moved to his own shop, he used to cut hair at a Brotherhood Barbershop on North Capitol and O. That's how we met. We've grown closer over the years. One of the ways we bonded was by taking road trips to Allenwood together to visit our uncles.

On one of those road trips to Allenwood in late 2011, Rico came along with me and my family, including Grandma, Uncle Alvin, Nikki and her son Dominique, and Kim. I requested Rico, Grandma, Doc, and Nikki requested Uncle Greg, Kim requested

Uncle Lo and Rico requested his uncle Darrin. With everyone in the visiting room together, at some point, I had a moment to step back and look at the scene. There was a man from both sides of my family, another one who married into the family, and a friend of the family, all incarcerated in the same place. Of course I knew this before being in the visiting room with all of them, but seeing them all together was striking. Three out of the four men, excluding my cousin Rico, were serving life sentences. It was one of those disturbing moments where I almost couldn't believe my eyes.

Sadly, this is not an uncommon scene in Washington, D.C. Not long before the above trip to Allenwood, I came across a July 2010 study from the Justice Policy Institute, which revealed the following:

- D.C. has the highest incarceration rate in the country and the third-highest rate of criminal justice control.
- Despite a 22 percent decrease in crime in D.C., from 2001 to 2009 arrests increased 9.4 percent during this time, mostly due to arrests for drug and nonviolent offenses.
- The greatest increases in arrests have been in Wards 5 and 7 (27 and 34 percent, respectively). These two wards have some of the highest percentages of people of color in the District and the highest unemployment rates.

- The number of women arrested in D.C. has increased 19 percent since 2001, including a 78 percent increase in drug arrests.
- Nine out of 10 people in D.C.'s Department of Corrections (DOC) are African American, despite only making up 54 percent of the total population.
- About 72 percent of men and 82 percent of women in the DOC are incarcerated for nonviolent offenses.
- Youth arrests have increased 42 percent from 2001 to 2009, mainly for misdemeanor offenses, which rose 183 percent during this time.
- About 96 percent of youth committed to the Department of Youth Rehabilitation Services (DYRS) are African American and 4 percent are Latino.

The study went on to show how D.C.'s spending demonstrates the prioritization of law enforcement over providing vital public programs and social support. This is further detailed with staggering homeless statistics and dismal public education scores. Every day, I see these kinds of numbers represented in flesh and blood. With our income inequality now the highest in the country, sometimes I feel like I'm on a train that's leaving its station destined for a better place and never to return. I'm on the train, at moments to my disbelief, but I can feel my feet firmly planted on its floor. I have a ticket and a designated seat, but I'm not sitting in it. I am in the very back of the train desperately trying to pull others on. They are like me and they should be on this train. They should have a chance to board. I'm holding onto them with all of my strength, struggling to get as many as I can on, but I'm running out of time. The train is starting to move.

That gathering in the visiting room at Allenwood full of family and friends was the last time I saw Uncle Greg. A couple of months later, after performing his cleaning duties in the cellblock, he hung himself in a small utility closet.

I cannot question my uncle's final prison sentence. He was a bank robber, convicted of the crime multiple times. Yet, he was far more than just that to us. And I miss him.

In 2010, along with four good friends, Alec, Mike, Kibwe, and Donald, I started an initiative called Sons of Life. Our mission is to mentor children of incarcerated parents and raise awareness about and for these children. The earliest seed for the group was planted on a visit to see my father. There was a boy in the visiting room who was about the same age I was when my father went away. I didn't approach the child, so I don't know the boy's name, but I'll never forget his face. Seeing him there in the way I used to made me walk away from that visit thinking I needed to do more. At the time, I was also in a serious relationship with a woman named Tiffany, and before that a woman named Kerry. Both had children with men who had been incarcerated at various points in their children's lives. I matured a great deal with these women, and I am deeply appreciative of how both stood by me through tough times. While we were together, I helped raise their children, and I often thought about the impact the fathers' incarceration had not only on their children's lives, but also on the lives of the mothers.

Before moving to CSOSA, I worked with Alec at Project Empowerment. Alec and I were both facilitators at PE, and he became one of my closest friends and confidants. Daily, we'd have great conversations about each other's lives and the fierceness of our city. Al came from a two-parent household that was very religious. But growing up his family also lived in an infamous apartment complex named Paradise Manor. Al did twelve years in prison, but upon his release, he completely turned his life around.

Al was the first person to really get me to working out seriously. In between sets and after our workouts together, we'd discuss doing some work in underserved communities beyond our jobs. Around the same time my lifelong friend, Mike, who was also from Hanover and whose father was serving a life sentence, approached me about getting more involved in the community. Simultaneously, my reformed younger homie Donald "Duck" Stevenson approached me. At the time, Duck's mother was incarcerated. Duck was from Sursum Corda, but I met him through his work as an outreach worker. Duck was passionate about starting something of our own. So with all the interest, we did. I brought in Kibwe a short while later. Kibwe's mother, Norma, was one of my mother's best friends. His father is serving a life sentence as well.

Immediately, the team set out to organize a Sons of Life toy drive. We all did the groundwork, along with my cousin Jason, registering children of incarcerated parents through various channels, and once the big day came, we were stunned at the outpouring of support. People from all over the D.C. area donated a mountain of toys, which we separated, wrapped, and distributed to the children. That first toy drive, along with an earlier turkey drive I led with the hip-hop artist Wale, Legreg Harrison, and the Board of Administration, sparked a series of very successful drives. My work with Sons of Life eventually exposed me to other causes and organizations in need of resources. To date, I've led a number of hunger drives, coat and clothes drives, drives for school supplies, and coordinated many other awareness and resource-raising events. Often, I will document the work I do on my own and with others in the community, not to bring attention to myself but to bring attention to the work and the need for it. I've found if you show people that you know what you're doing and why it matters, they will be more inclined to participate.

Now I was working with ex-offenders at CSOSA and had a firm commitment to my community work off the clock. At CSOSA, I was given a lot of responsibility early, but it took some time for my colleagues to get used to my style. They'd see me embracing our clients and didn't quite understand it. They questioned the informal appearance of my interactions with them. Some even questioned how I could show such affection, a tight handshake and a hug, with clients that had been convicted of murder. CSOSA supervises people on parole, probation, and supervised release. We know our clients' full criminal history and the crimes they were convicted for before being released to us. This, in addition to a professional protocol for our industry, created a barrier for most of my colleagues. It's understandable. They didn't come up the way I did. I knew our clients' land and their language. I also happened to know personally many of the clients that came through our doors. For those I did not know, I'd still immediately see their humanity.

Over time, my colleagues saw that though I had a cordial and informal appearance with our clients, I was effective. Their chance at freedom was both personal and professional for me, and I expected the most from them. I'm tough on my guys. I give hugs and handshakes, but I also speak hard truths and give them straight talk. I'm always disappointed when guys get released and don't do what they're supposed to do. Their behavior is a poor reflection on their peers and makes my job harder. Still, for every ex-offender who doesn't take his release seriously or gets back into the life, there are ten who are trying to do all the right things and just need opportunities to continue to grow and improve their lives, but you often don't hear about them. This is one of the reasons I work so hard. Redemption and the transformation of the spirit is a sight to behold, and when the media spotlight finds its way to me, often I redirect it to shine on them.

With Ford Motor Company, comedian Steve Harvey puts on an annual national award show in Las Vegas called the Neighborhood Awards (formerly the Hoodie Awards). The show honors local businesses, religious/neighborhood leaders, churches, and high schools from all over the country for their contributions as well as excellence within their own neighborhoods. Four nominees are honored in multiple categories and a winner is selected from each; at the end of the night a grand prize goes to the winner of best community leader. In 2011, to my great surprise, I became one of the four nominees for best community leader and later was selected the winner of the category. When comedian Kevin Hart announced me the winner, I rose from my seat in complete shock and moved to the stage to receive my award. When I got to the podium, I looked out at the sea of people. It didn't seem like such a large crowd when I was sitting down, but being up there I saw the full view of the twelve thousand some-odd people in the Mandalay Bay event center. I didn't have a speech prepared, as I truly didn't expect to win. I was young and up against stiff competition from nominees from New York City. So standing at the podium, I just opened my mouth and spoke from my heart.

I commend Steve Harvey and Ford Motor Company for recognizing those of us who do the best we can with what we have, working in communities who seem to have so little. In terms of resources, we do have little, but what we lack in that area we make up for with our resolve. I was happy to be selected for the award, but, again, receiving attention for the work I do is not why I do it. I do it because I can't stand to see suffering in the ghetto, especially suffering children. I do it for the vast expanse of wasted minds, wasted for not knowing better, for never learning better, and not knowing why or how to get better. I do it for the demonstration of alternatives to crime, alternatives to getting by on instincts born out of survival. I do it for love and because my family loved me so much. Not knowing better, just wanting better, wanting better for me, then getting caught up in the web of humanity, caught between agency, power and principality. It was my family who first showed me how to love others.

A couple of months after the award show, an unfathomable opportunity came to me. A prison forum was being held at FCI Cumberland, where my father is imprisoned. I'd be representing CSOSA there, along with a panel of representatives from other government agencies and non-profit organizations. A large number of inmates from D.C. were to be released soon, and each panelist would take ten to fifteen minutes to speak on the various resources they had available for them upon release. My father wasn't being paroled, but inmates are allowed to attend various prison programs of their choosing, and he would be present at the forum. A dream had come true.

My father had missed so much, so many moments of my life. He watched me grow, but only intermittently, first from a great distance and later much closer. But what he saw and heard from me always happened within the confines of a prison visiting room. When I became an adult, we'd talk about my work, and I'd do my best to describe to him what it looked like. We hoped that he'd one day get to see me in action, but we couldn't see it happening, not with his sentence in the way. The closest he ever came to seeing me in freedom was a live television interview I gave on D.C.'s Fox News affiliate for my Neighborhood Award nomination. The city responded incredibly in their vote for me, and that interview certainly helped with that response.

I was emotional. I pictured my father watching me in the TV room making everyone be quiet. He was seeing me in my daily world—live—outside the parameters of a visiting room. Trying to remain poised, I thought about him the entire time. I acknowledged him, smiling and saying to the program's host, Allison Seymour, "My father's watching..." It was a big moment for us, but it was small compared to the opportunity we had coming up. Life kept opening up for me. Now I was speaking on behalf of a federal government agency, which I never saw happening, and I certainly didn't see me speaking at my father's prison. It was improbable. CSOSA didn't select me because my father was there. It was the most beautiful happenstance.

When the big day came, I put on my best suit, shirt, and tie and met up with the delegation of panelists. We all rode to Cumberland together in a fifteen-passenger van. The two hour-plus ride to the prison couldn't have gone any smoother. It was unlike any other prison trip I had ever taken. When we arrived, I immediately took the lead in helping my fellow panelists navigate the admittance process at Cumberland. I assisted a number of them to complete their visitation forms and, when we were all finished, I collected them. I then handed the stack of applications to the officer, sat down, and waited patiently with the others. But as panelist after panelist was called and cleared, I remained seated. Something had to be wrong. I had been visiting prisons long enough to know how the process worked. My application was on top of the rest, so I should have been one of the first to be cleared. I tried to remain cool. I knew any sign of frustration would only hurt the situation. Be cooperative. *Yeah, but what is going on? What's the problem? Why has everyone else cleared but me?*

The prison's database had a list of all the inmates who registered to attend the forum, and when they ran my name through the computer I came up on my father's visiting list. This was unprecedented. How could I be a panelist, a guest of the prison, and come up on a prisoner's guest list? It was cause for concern, a conundrum, and I immediately became a security risk. But I knew none of this at the time. All of my fellow panelists had disappeared from sight. And I stood there alone, trying to explain the situation and receiving only stone-faced stares in response. A half an hour had passed. "I'm not going to get in," I thought. "They're not going to let me through. The program is going to begin without me. Where is my father? Is he sitting in the auditorium? Yes, he's there. What will they tell him? What can I do?"

Increasingly, it appeared there was nothing that I could do. I had showed all my identification and had explained the situation as clearly as I possibly could to no avail. I didn't know that while I had been detained, the associate warden had pulled my father out of the auditorium. Face to face, my father explained the situation to him. With his explanation, my clearance, and the corroboration of my story, I was admitted.

Given the situation, I was slotted to speak last. I sat on stage, trying to be as professional as I could be, appearing to be listening to my fellow panelists with great interest. But my father was right there. Like I imagined, he had a front row seat. He and I kept making eye contact and sharing knowing smiles throughout the presentations. It was fantastic. Then my moment to speak came, and standing up and walking over to the podium I, again, composed myself. I wanted to give my best presentation for inmates who might use our services and the best performance for my father.

Not long into my presentation, I noticed my dad's hands were to his face. His head was down and his back was shaking. He wept uncontrollably, crying through my entire presentation. It was just the second time I had seen him cry. Only these were tears of joy. We were together in a way we thought we never would be. It was the closest we had been to freedom since he went to prison.

As a child, I went from seeing my father every day to seeing him a total of three times in thirteen years while he was incarcerated in Lompoc. We just couldn't afford to visit him. D.C.

doesn't have a state prison, so offenders from D.C. are managed by the Federal Bureau of Prisons, which can place them anywhere in the country. It can be as close as a couple of hours away in Maryland or as far as California. For many poor families, having a family member locked up just a couple of states over is like having that family member across the country.

More attention needs to be given to the impact that mass incarceration has had on black communities. When you take a million plus men away, making them members of a brutally unforgiving system, you're not just taking them off the streets. When you institutionalize them forever, whether behind bars or scarred for life with the mark of criminal, you're taking them away from their families—their children—and their communities. The emotional, psychological, and economic effect this has had on impoverished communities of color is immeasurable. You have millions of young men and women who are poor, undereducated, and growing up without adult males in their homes and in their communities. I'm talking entire neighborhoods with scant evidence of grown men. It's not natural. It causes deep confusion for the affected families and depressive corrosion of the community.

This is what has happened and is happening. Today, the story of poor blacks in the U.S. can be found in deindustrialization, poor education, and America's system of mass incarceration.

In addition to not living a relatively balanced life, a life where a child can look and see and know where they came from, the emotional, psychological, and economic blow dealt to these families has made it unbelievably hard for them to compete. Now the playing field has expanded. In this age, we're competing with the world. But how can you compete with the world when the fundamental unit of the family and the community has been systematically and indefinitely taken apart? Men and women must work together to start this upward momentum. It's the way it always has been and the way it always will be. Any society that fails to understand that or lacks the ability to leverage that dynamic is lost.

When you commit a crime, you should have to pay for that crime. After the time is served, an ex-offender should be able to come back to his family and his community and be an asset to it. Reintegration into society shouldn't be easy, but it also shouldn't be an impossible task. There needs to be more hope for the ex-offender, more forgiveness and flexibility from the system that judged them and from the society into which they return. This is the work I do, and I've seen success stories, but there are not nearly enough. Reformed ex-offenders, particularly black and brown men who possess an unwavering willingness to work and be productive members of society, ought to be able to more regularly transform their lives and reintegrate into society.

Isn't this America?

What happened to the dream?

Today the poor remain poor, the criminals remain criminals, and most couldn't care less about their condition. This indifference is in actuality an outright rejection of the American ideal.

235

We've always been a nation fighting to be better. There's always been a diverse and powerful resistance of people who stood against obstinate discrimination and injustice of all kinds here. It made America worthy of existence and justified our grand democratic experiment. Yet today, mostly, there's great apathy in the presence of great subterfuge, a terrible proposition.

But I'm going to keep fighting and keep making noise, right around the giant's ear. And one of these days he's going to hear me.

A New Generation,
A New Mission

I'm staring up at the dark morning sky, feeling the insistent chill that has settled throughout my body. For the moment, everyone around me is at rest. The execs are burrowed inside their sleeping bags, and a security guard is patrolling the parking lot. I reach for my phone; it is 4:00 a.m. and 30 degrees. We've been outside for six hours now.

Putting my phone down, I sit up and run my hand over my cardboard bed. I'm stiff, but this cardboard has actually made a difference. I rolled off it a few times during the night and felt the concrete, cold and hard, against my face. Jokingly, I complained about the conditions when we first lay down, but I know the night we just spent outside is luxurious compared to what children without shelter go through. I understand better now.

When I leave this spot, I'm going to return to a warm, comfortable shower, and certainty of direction. I'm cold, but not nearly as cold as I could be. Love, knowing that I'm loved, that I have been loved, warmed me throughout the night. It has warmed me throughout my life, especially during my adolescence when each day the confusion of my circumstance and fierceness of my environment worked to weaken the warmth of my heart. Now my greatest wish is that any child in distress—

children all over the world, but especially those engulfed in the madness of this city—somehow finds the kind of love that kept me, the sense of security that carried me through. They absolutely need that. If in some way I could guarantee a distressed child's peace and security by my spending a night outside, I would gladly do so every night.

For now, though, it's just one night. Still, I hope, in some small way, doing this makes a difference.

The night began with a candlelight vigil for homelessness on the grounds of Covenant House Washington, D.C. There are Covenant houses spread throughout the Americas. Their mission is to help homeless youth escape the streets. I was invited to be one of the speakers at the vigil and decided that I'd also sleep out to help raise awareness.

The crowd was comprised of Covenant House residents, workers, and various people from the D.C. area, including the group of executives designated to sleep out. After the vigil, we all moved inside the building for the second part of the evening. Inside, we listened to heartfelt words via satellite from the CEO of Covenant House in New York City and watched few presentations including one from a Pulitzer Prize–winning journalist who had helped write a noted book on homeless youth. We were then separated into small groups, seated at round tables, and encouraged to share our stories through a series of activities. I participated for a while but was pulled away from the table by old friends who lived close by and had heard I was going to be in the area.

In the building's entrance, my little friend Kanye, all three feet of him standing by his grandmother's side, greeted me, saying, "Tony, where's my *D.C. or Nothing* t-shirt?" I couldn't have been happier; his spunk was back. His eyes were bright and alive again, and he had fully recovered from his prior serious illness.

Kanye's father was one of my first mentees nearly ten years ago when I was a roving leader for the city. I still keep in touch with the family, which is how I found out that Kanye was sick. For a while, we didn't know if he was going to make it. I went to visit him in the hospital and found that he had been rejecting his medication. I observed the nurses trying to give him the medicine through a syringe and figured that it probably looked scary to him. I asked them to pour it into one of those little cups. When they did, I took a sip and asked him if he'd take a sip just like me, and he did.

I was glad that they had come to see me at the event. They were one of my first outreach families, and thankfully they were doing well. There were three boys in the family, and now the middle son had a child of his own, a bright and brash little boy who had a better chance because his father was there for him and was working toward greater positive possibilities.

When I returned to my small group, the evening was coming to a close. A short while later, a few of my friends and I joined the group of D.C. area executives who had chosen to sleep outside for the night. In addition to us, there were about eight others who decided to sleep out. Once all the participants moved outside, everyone but my group of guys quickly positioned themselves atop their cardboard pallets and into their sleeping bags. One of the sleepers situated closest to me and my group started snoring loudly not long after lying down. Standing with my group, we cracked a few jokes and laughed about it, but the man kept on undisturbed, sleeping and snoring as if he were at home in his bed. I snore, too, so we probably formed an inharmonious duet when I finally closed my eyes.

But for the rest of us, sleep was still far off. I was surrounded by good company, and the spirit of the event enlivened me. The three guys that came with me shared the same energy. The four of us stood off to the side in pairs, talking, sharing, and laughing. While we talked, I observed the group dynamics apart from us. I didn't give it much thought, but it was interesting to see we were the only ones up and conversing. Everyone else had positioned themselves inside their sleeping bags. I wondered what the other sleepers' stories were. Aside from the ice-breaking activities, I didn't get a chance to really connect with anyone new inside.

Getting colder, but warmed by the spirit of possibility, my little group kept up our conversation while standing among the sleepers. At some point, one of the participants sat up in his sleeping bag and said to us "Could you guys keep it down? There are others trying to rest, you know."

I was taken aback by the comment but made sure that we lowered our tone. Later I learned that someone, perhaps the same guy, sent a message complaining about our "noisemaking" to the director of Covenant House. Given we were all sleeping out in solidarity with homeless youth, the whole noisemaking comment was curious. We weren't disturbing anyone in the group. The snoring man definitely didn't have a problem with us, and he lay the closest. Still, I wonder how many shared the opinion. I wondered, while we all were snuggled in our sleeping bags, how much the others considered the noises and the dangerous element of uncertainty that homeless children endured nightly. One of the reasons we were out there was to attempt to approach the feeling of what it meant to be homeless. It wasn't supposed to be a pleasant sleep.

For me, this event wasn't just some experience that I'd be a part of and then go talk about at dinner parties. And I wasn't out there doing it to feel better about myself. I was out there to serve and be selfless. But, given our appearance, I believe he had stereotyped us and lashed out at us. Coming over to us would have been more productive. We could have learned from each other. In coming closer to us, speaking to us, he would have discovered that the so-called noise was in actuality a form of celebration. We were rejoicing. Look at the beauty of us coming together, everyone, but specifically my guys. We are young men who very much understand the plight of the children that come to Covenant House. We were once them, in a sense, given the extremes of our childhoods. Now, thankfully, we had the stability and the consciousness to voluntarily put ourselves in a sleeping bag and spend a cold night outside. But before lying down, we chose to stand and celebrate each other's presence. We were alive – alive with all our wits and a good measure of warmth left. Our stories could have easily turned out differently. So our ever-present history demanded we share some laughter. Those who are on the frontline understand the need for lightheartedness. It lifts spirits and staves off the menacing beginnings of insanity. It diminishes the weight that constantly presses down given all that you've been through and all that you see, daily, in the struggle.

Watching and attending sporting events is another way I relieve stress from my work. I still love boxing, and as I've gotten older, I've grown to appreciate the rich history of the sport. For blacks, particularly in the first three quarters of the twentieth century, champion fighters were far more than sportsmen and entertainers. They represented triumph and hope. They were symbols of greater possibilities, heroic figures that fought with the everyday struggles of their race of people in mind. From Jack Johnson to Joe Louis and later Muhammad Ali, what these fighters achieved in and outside the ring helped to influence and change in our country.

Today the sport is much maligned for its splintered state of affairs. There are many factors that contributed to its precipitous decline, but for the true boxing fan, the sport lives on. The buzz isn't nearly as large as it once was, and the names aren't, either, but witnessing the science and the heart in one of those explosive sequences of combination and connection is still a thing of beauty.

I was looking forward to doing that very thing when I took a group of my Sons of Life mentees to the D.C. Convention Center to watch the Ty Barnett fight. Named for Washington D.C.'s first home rule mayor, the Walter E. Washington Convention Center is a sprawling two million square foot building set in the heart of the Shaw community. Not all D.C. neighborhoods have the proud history that Shaw has, yet its recent transformation is emblematic of a change happening in neighborhoods all over the District.

As I presented the tickets for the boys at the gates and we all entered the building, I couldn't help but be impressed by the place even though I had been there a few times before. The boys were impressed, too, putting their heads back, looking up, and gawking at the high ceilings. Watching them for a moment, a thought occurred to me: this big beautiful building and the kind of change that came with it will certainly impact the boys' lives, and not necessarily in a good way. Shaking the thought off and telling myself we were there to enjoy the fight, I gathered everyone and led the group to our seats.

Each boy was the child of an incarcerated parent. Two were my family members, cousins Brian and Taquan. Another pair were brothers, Delfon and Xavier, and the fifth and youngest boy's name was Mark Anthony. Mark Anthony has an amazing personality that shines right through his severe ADHD. He refers to me by my full name, which cracks me up every time, and he can talk with the best of them; the boy's mouth goes and the rest of his body follows. So with that, and the fact that he was by far the youngest of our party, I had to be sure to keep my eye on him in the convention center.

The ADHD medication Mark Anthony takes suppresses his appetite, so during the week he doesn't eat a lot. His mother doesn't give him his medicine during the weekend, so he eats a lot then. We had all eaten earlier at my house before going to the fight, so everybody was still and content sitting in their seats—but not Mark Anthony. Boldly, he declared, "Tony Lewis, I'm hungry. I want some nachos *and* a hot dog." Smiling, I got up and motioned for him to follow me.

At the concession stand, Mark Anthony bobbed and danced in anticipation of getting his food. When the food arrived, we headed back to our seats. As we were walking, Mark Anthony turned to me with the most sincere face I'd ever seen and said, "Tony Lewis, do you miss your Dad like I miss mine?"

I couldn't believe it. I felt tears welling up in my eyes and I answered him, "I do."

I was once him, and today I am still the child of an incarcerated parent. It's been a lifelong fight for me.

Epilogue: D.C. or Nothing

I n 1996, I was introduced to the music of Jay Z through the song "Can I Live." That song and the entire *Reasonable Doubt* album forever changed hip-hop for me. It made the music personal. It made me feel closer to those I had lost. "This is my past he's rhyming about," I thought as I listened. I'd sit transfixed, marveling at his precision, the nuance, and the naming of things. He rhymed in a code that, long before the book *Decoded*, I quickly decoded for myself. In those early days, I tried to share my excitement for his music with my peers, but they couldn't see it yet. But I did, I saw it so very clearly and, honestly, his music made the trials I endured daily a little bit easier. It made me feel as if someone out there understood me, my block, and my family. And he had made it. If he could make it, so could I.

Because of the strong influence of go-go music in D.C., and to some extent D.C.'s rivalry with street dudes from New York City, generally we were uninterested in hip-hop at the start. While future hip-hop artists from other major cities were listening to the vanguard music with great interest and slowly developing their own culture and sound around it, we were not. As a result, we didn't have a breakout D.C. hip-hop act nationally until the early 2000s. By that time, Jay Z was well on his way to breaking the record for number one albums, and hip-hop had become the greatest cultural force since jazz.

Seeing hip-hop create service and security jobs in big cities like New York, Los Angeles, and Atlanta, I dreamt of a vigorous hip-hop culture in D.C. where ex-offenders could more easily find work. There were many ex-offenders coming home to an entirely different Washington D.C., where jobs increasingly were available only for a highly skilled work force. Additionally, with D.C. being a federal city, government jobs were plentiful, but you had to be qualified and not have a felony.

Part of my hopes for a better hip-hop culture in D.C. was also about young people. Hip-hop had become a bigger dream in the hood than sports. You didn't have to be big, tall, strong or fast. Anyone could rhyme, and I wanted to encourage dreaming. I wanted to encourage the young people to tell their stories and be proud of where they come from. No other outlet presented a better opportunity of expression for them. You might think these young people should be aspiring to be doctors, lawyers, and businessmen, not hip-hop artists, and, generally, they should, but realistically, the way big cities are today, they don't see these professionals in their communities. It's extremely hard to aspire to be something that you have no model for. Eventually, you can work to become a professional—look at me—but something else has to come first. First there has to be a dream of some kind, some kind of connection where the constructive habits and focus of success are formed. Then if your first dream falters, you know you have the stuff it takes to make a new one and work toward making that dream come true.

I knew as a young professional just hitting my stride that I had little influence over and little connection with those who drove D.C.'s economy. I did, however, have some influence in the street, which is almost always the birthplace and driver of great hip-hop. To get an industry running in D.C., we had to get our local hip-hop artists some support and exposure. At the time, Wale showed the most promise, and we met through a mutual friend right before he released his first album. Now he's a Grammy-nominated artist and owner of a number one record on the Billboard charts for his album *The Gifted*, but on his way up he wasn't getting the support he deserved around the city.

Wale had lived in D.C. as a child, but his formative years were spent in Maryland. Due to its beginnings, authenticity and street credibility in hip-hop meant a lot. To ascend, you have to be from a big city, or the big city where you reside must embrace you as one of their own. A great example of this is found with the rapper Drake. At the start, Drake represented his city, Toronto, unabashedly and often. Now on the landscape of hip-hop, Toronto was far from New York City, Los Angeles, Chicago, Houston, and New Orleans and Atlanta. Those cities are familiar hubs of hip-hop, and Toronto was not, but it was enough. Drake was smart. He understood the culture.

While Wale won the city over with his prodigious talent, I embraced him. D.C. needed him as much as he needed D.C., and I needed him to be the pioneer that he appeared he could be. He was our hope and he was my hope for my grandiose visions of a hip-hop culture in D.C. Kids needed to be inspired, and guys coming home needed jobs. A movement could start with one artist.

Talent was never the issue in D.C. The issue was focus and solidarity. Early in Wale's career, I gladly squashed petty beefs directed at him and promoted him whenever and however I could, trying to build local support. One night, out of frustration at all the fracturing and hate in the city, I came up with the phrase "D.C. or Nothing." I hoped it would be a slogan that we could all rally around. I started saying it and promoting it without explanation or definition, hoping that, as I am hoping here, that listeners would find meaning in it for themselves. Slowly, the city started recognizing the importance of supporting our local hip-hop artist, and many of them did so under the banner "D.C. or Nothing."

The city doesn't yet have a robust music industry where ex-offenders can more easily find work, but the culture is getting there and other artists are being signed and good music is being made. Something positive is established for young people of forgotten communities to connect with. Now I need other industries and professionals to come along.

Though I could have moved years ago, I still live in the same house on Hanover that I grew up in. It was a conscious choice that I made early in my career. The demographics on Hanover didn't change until recently. The surrounding area has gentrified as well, but there's still a heavy concentration of long-term residents who happen to be poor and black. I made my decision to stay when Hanover was far more like the old one than the new one, and I did it because I wanted my neighbors and the neighborhood to see me getting up and going to work every day. I wanted to be the guy in the neighborhood I didn't see as a child. I wanted to be accessible. And I am. There's no soapbox in front of my house, and I don't carry one around with me either. It's where I'm from, and it's easy to be natural. However, when appropriate, I do find myself having conversations, with the young people of the neighborhood especially, about things beyond what we see in front of us. This isn't revolutionary, but them seeing me present, having access to me, and seeing me caring about my community, together with others doing the same thing, could be the beginning of a revolution.

A couple of years ago, one of my neighborhood's new residents became a victim of gun violence. Being a new resident, it went without saying that the victim was innocent. But so was an old resident that had been gunned down in much the same manner a couple of weeks before. The media firestorm for the new resident was unlike anything I had ever seen around Hanover. Innocent people had been dying in our area for years. I mourned the loss of the new resident and the old resident equally, but the city didn't respond with the same kind of integrity. Two innocent people from the same neighborhood were murdered in the span of two weeks. For one resident there's a loud citywide outcry, for the other there's silence. Was the new resident's life more valuable than the old resident's?

I'm talking rich and poor here. Black and white. I'm talking the value of human life and the values of a city divided. There are some who hold more important titles, whose impact on society and culture create more ripples in death. But not one human life is more valuable than another. Not one.

Marches in and of themselves don't change much. Today, unless the numbers are really great, they contribute even less toward stirring consciousness and raising awareness, which is the march's primary function. Those who plan and participate in marches should know this. The daily work of changing minds, hearts, and policies through varying other strategies are far more effective. Knowing this, but feeling the need to create an immediate response to the contrasting coverage of the two deaths in my neighborhood, I coordinated a march for peace along with my good friend Silas Grant. We had streets blocked off and police escorts as we marched around the area of the two shootings. We prepared many signs with some of them reading, "D.C. or Nothing." In an instant, the slogan had taken on a new meaning.

Recently, after a multiple shooting at Tyler House, Silas and I organized a second march for peace. In the first march for peace, I was encouraged by the number of young people that turned out, especially the most unlikely characters. In our second march for peace, they showed up again, but this time we also had a much wider range of demographics, native Washingtonians and new residents to the city, government officials and griots of the ghetto, rich and poor and people of many different ethnicities. The groundwork was paying off. With knowledge and respect for each other's cultures and particular circumstance, and a willingness to listen to difference of opinion, we can come together.

Not long ago, I was invited to be the guest speaker at Gonzaga's mother/son celebration. For twenty-eight years, the Gonzaga Mother's Club has been putting on this annual spring event. The Mother's Club is an elegant force and an essential part of Gonzaga's rich tradition. I was surprised and humbled by the invitation to speak at my alma mater. It was a great honor; I understood immediately the company it placed me in. On the day of the event, I was very nervous, but when it came time for me to speak I settled in. I shared with the congregation an abbreviated version of my life. I talked about my time at Gonzaga and the guiding principles I learned there, and I talked about my parents. Without going into the severity of my mother's illness, I alluded to it in parts throughout the speech. In honoring Grandma and Aunt Bonnie, who were at the celebration supporting me together with my love, Jessica, I told the gathering that my mother couldn't make it. She could not make the event, but she made the dream. She fashioned it, put it in me, and made it so that the spirit of her love could help me see the dream through. I was standing there because of her.

After the speech, a number of the mothers came up to me and said they hoped that their sons would grow into a men like me. Like me? I was stunned. Here I was in a place that was once alien to me, surrounded by people who were wealthy and from wholly different cultures, and I was being told that. I learned something very important in that moment.

At heart, I'm still Slugg from Hanover. I couldn't foresee any of the good things that have happened to me, but as doors open and people continue to embrace me, I embrace them back. I want them to get to know me and understand that there are hundreds of thousands of people like me in this country. I refuse to be the anomaly. Those of you who are from a tough place, embrace and believe in your divine power. Through faith and work, you can make it. Those who've had an easier start should believe the same. Yet, I believe to whom much is given, much is required. Our society has grown too callous and cynical. Indifference has become one of the worst kinds of oppression. By working purposefully and with some positive feeling for the people on the other side of the divide, we can come together to live better, brighter, and more enriched lives.

My daughter, Isabella Marie Lewis, was born on October 17, 2013. In 2007, my daughter Korry Samone Lewis died shortly after birth. Her death was so painful for me I can't even find the words to express it. There was a void left in me when Korry passed, and I think about her all the time. Now with Isabella, I've never been more motivated. By working to help the Mark Anthonys of the world, I know that I'll also be helping my Isabella. I must do all that I can to make the world a better place for her and the generation she was born into. But I'm also very much aware of how important it is to be a good father, to be present, to be there every day to love her, to guide her, and to supply her with every need. Her dreams are my dreams, and I will be there to support her and to encourage her and to do all I can to help make her dreams come true. I will never leave her, never, not until God takes me.

Acknowledgments

I have been blessed to encounter so many people that have made positive contributions to my life that it's going to be impossible to thank everyone. So I would like to start by saying "Thank You Everyone" (laugh). To my FAMILY, there is no me without you. To my wife, my daughter, my parents, grandparents, aunts, uncles, and cousins—I love you all immensely. You are my core, my base, my foundation, my motivation. Thank you for everything; I hope I have made you proud.

I want to thank all my comrades from Hanover/1st–N-O/NCO. I love each and every one of you. Young and old, you are like my family. I could never express what you mean to me. I will never forget you or outgrow you. I want for you what I want for myself. RIP LIL CHARLES, LIL DENNIS, BIG DENNIS, FAT JOHN, ALAN, FAT MIKE, TIM, BROCK, SCOOP, JUNE, TAY, and MALLY.

Love and respect to Florida Park, 3rd-N-P, Bates Street, Sursum Cordas (The U, Sibley Plaza, Temple Court, The Market), Tyler House , 5th-N-O, KDP,1512, 1st Street, Lincoln Rd. I want to thank my beloved city ...The District of Columbia...All four quadrants: NW, SE, NE, and SW, every crew, every neighborhood, thanks for inspiring me, encouraging me, supporting me, challenging me, teaching me, and nurturing me into who I have become. I love you. To all of the fallen in DC, all of you who died prematurely in these streets, we celebrate your life and not your death. This book is dedicated to you and all your infinite potential. Your spirit lives on, you are still here, your presence is felt daily.

I appreciate all of the people that I have stood on the front lines with over the past fifteen years trying to help people have a better life. All of the community-based organizations that have put it all on the line for those that need it the most in DC, like Cease Fire, Don't Smoke the Brothers and Sisters, The Alliance of Concerned Men, Peaceoholics, All of the Family Support Collaborative's, Dreamworks, and many other nonprofit partners I have encountered over the years, thank you . To all of the faith-based institutions that are truly committed to serving the people, I salute you. To every roving leader, every person at the D.C. Department of Parks and Recreation, every person at the D.C. Department of Employment Services, every person at Project Empowerment, every person at College Bound, and every person at the Court Services and Offender Supervision Agency that I have had the pleasure and honor of serving with, I am eternally grateful for the experiences I have had with you.

To the people that have trusted me enough, valued me enough, and respected me enough to let me into their lives to assist them in any way, I have infinite appreciation for you. You have taught me so much about life and about myself. My interactions with you have made me a better father, son, friend, husband, and an overall better man. If I have interacted with you as a facilitator, mentor, job coach, job developer, speaker, community organizer or in any other capacity, I want to say thank you. Your confidence in me is what allowed me to have confidence in myself. You fuel me daily, and I will never stop fighting for you. What we have shared will always be with me. Your accomplishments will always be my greatest accomplishments for we are forever intertwined.

To the coauthor of this book, Kevin L. Reeves, it was an honor and a pleasure to collaborate with you on this book. You are one of the most passionate, articulate, and intelligent people I know. I have so much respect for you as a writer, an author, and as a man. My level of appreciation for who you are and what you have meant to this process cannot be summed up in words. You will always have my deepest appreciation and gratitude. I cannot wait for the world to find out what I already know. Thanks for embarking on this journey with me, my brother. Thank You to Jeff Ourvan for believing in this book and what it represented, I appreciate you. Thank You to Rafeena Ahmad and Joanne Asala for your contributions to this book.

RIP CHUCK BROWN
RIP MARION BARRY

Undying Respect,
Slugg

257

Made in the USA
Columbia, SC
04 November 2023

25469766R00155